Martin

The P

Heroic Bloodshed

with contributions from:
John Ashbrook
John Costello
Martin Coxhead
Paul Duncan
Steve Holland
Michelle Le Blanc
Colin Odell

www.pocketessentials.com

First published in Great Britain 2000 by Pocket Essentials, 18 Coleswood Rd, Harpenden, Herts, AL5 1EQ

Distributed in the U.S.A. by Trafalgar Square Publishing, P.O.Box 257, Howe Hill Rd, North Pomfret, Vermont 05053

A CIP catalogue record for this book is available from the British Library.

ISBN 1-903047-0?-?

9 8 7 6 5 4 3 2 1

Book typeset by DP Fact & Fiction.
Printed and bound by Cox & Wyman

for Claude

Acknowledgements

My thanks to John Ashbrook, John Costello, Martin Coxhead, Paul Duncan, Steve Holland, Michelle Le Blanc, Colin Odell for supplying text, to Made In Hong Kong, MIA and Eastern Heroes for supplying videos, and to John Woo, Wong Kar-Wai and Christopher Doyle for supplying their time. Most of all, thanks to Claude, who shot me through the heart 3 years ago - I hope I never recover.

Note

Much of this text originally appeared in Crime Time 7, *edited by Paul Duncan, and has been updated by Martin Fitzgerald with Paul's permission. The Wong Kar-Wai/Christopher Doyle interview first appeared in* Crime Time 5, *and was expanded for publication in the* Crime Time Filmbook *(ed John Ashbrook, 1997, No Exit Press).*

Contents

Heroic Bloodshed: Shot To Death?
by Martin Fitzgerald

The kung fu movies of Bruce Lee have been popular in the West since their release in the mid-70s. Then super-acrobat and super-stuntguy Jackie Chan superseded him in the 80s. Since 1991, when John Woo's *The Killer* was released in the West, interest has grown in the gangster action films of Hong Kong - generically known as Heroic Bloodshed. Several video labels have centred their output on these gangster flicks and an increasing number of magazines and books have been published containing background information on the subject.

This Pocket Essential, which contains interviews, articles and reviews, is an introduction to this wild and confusing world where singers are the top actors, where stories and stunts are made up as they go along, and where only the subtitles are faster than the bullets.

Checking The Clip

What is Heroic Bloodshed? It is a phrase coined by writer/fan Rick Baker after he saw John Woo's *A Better Tomorrow* (1986). It is used to distinguish between Hong Kong gangster gun operas and the traditional kung fu opuses. Basically in Heroic Bloodshed there are bullets flying across the screen instead of feet. This results in blood, carnage, cars wrecked, family honour insulted and avenged, drugs taken, buildings on fire, war, dead bodies strewn across the streets, and very bad men doing unmentionable things.

But before we explore the films, let's explore the place where they are made.

Hong Kong is separated into Hong Kong Island, Kowloon (a Peninsula on the mainland) and The New Territories (north of Kowloon, on the border with China). There are 6 million inhabitants, 3 million on the island and the other 3 million on the mainland. As the population increased, the urban areas of Kowloon spread into the New Territories, whilst the island had nowhere to go but up. Divided by water, there is also a cultural divide - the island is Westernised, has lots of bars and night life, whilst the mainland is still very much influenced by traditional Chinese culture and values.

Every global industry is targeting Hong Kong, Taiwan and Singapore because of the large number of cheap workers with formidable technology skills. Offices and factories are being set up in

Hong Kong, Kuala Lumpur and Singapore. And where there is commerce, there are the triads.

The triads are a secret criminal organisation who specialise in drugs, money laundering, robbery and anything else that suits their opportunistic nature. There are about a dozen active triad gangs in Hong Kong and, unlike the way they are portrayed in the movies, they like to control things in secret. (Originally, the triads were a network of secret Chinese political movements, formed in the 17th century. By the time their political ambitions were achieved in 1911, their surreptitious machinations had already been adapted by some for more nefarious objectives.) They are an underground operation and Westerners have very little contact with them. Basically, if you spot a man with a lot of tattoos over his body, the odds are that he is a triad soldier.

An important Chinese concept is face (respect). If you ask a Chinese person to explain something to you and, once he has, you still do not understand, if you ask him to repeat it, he would very probably take that as a loss of face. It would not be your fault for not understanding, it would be his fault for not explaining it properly, and you would have insulted him by stating as much. The face issue is a very important part of the culture. The triads play on this concept of face: it is a sort of emotional blackmail. A great loss of face is to go to the police and report a triad for threatening behaviour. Therefore, a lot of the crime is tolerated and ignored because the populace want to keep the matter quiet. The triads are never spoken about, but they are there. Always. They remain because they operate at a level where they are tolerated. They are annoying enough to turn a profit, but not so annoying that the authorities clamp down on them.

Bullet-Point: Brother - Triad members often refer to each other as brothers, and the senior member is often called 'big brother.' These affectionate terms emphasise the family aspect of the triads.

Loading

It would be remiss to mention at this point that the triads are involved in the film business. They have an annoying habit of being producers and, when they want a star for a role in a film, it is not unknown for the star to be kidnapped, raped, beaten up or whatever until they agree to play the role. And I'm not talking about small-fry here. Although Jackie Chan has been immune because of his standing in the industry, Andy Lau, Anita Mui, Jet Li, Chow Yun Fat and many others have had managers shot dead and other frightening incidents to contend with.

The triads are so involved with local politics, police and commerce that it is impossible to extricate them from the film industry, or the society. However, some maintain that their involvement is not all bad. A few of the triad film producers try to make art films in an attempt to win international prestige and awards - which gains them a lot of face. Also, since the triads are preoccupied with the idea of honour and face, that is generally the subject of the films they produce.

But why did the triads want to get involved in the first place? The reason was that in the late-80s film-makers like Tsui Hark and John Woo completely re-invented the Hong Kong cinema, injected it with energy and vitality, and Hong Kongers queued up to get as much of it as they could. Smelling the money, the triads wanted their cut.

Although there is still triad involvement in the Hong Kong film industry, most of them have left to make their money elsewhere. The reason? The box-office popularity of Heroic Bloodshed only boomed for 10 years. There is now less quick money to be made because the home-grown filmmakers are being ignored in favour of American blockbusters.

Safety Off

When the pro-gangster movies began to appear in the wake of John Woo's *A Better Tomorrow*, there was a rush of youngsters wanting to join the triads. After making a few more films glorifying the role of honourable villains, Woo declared that his 1992 master-piece *Hard-Boiled* was constructed so that both heroes were cops. He hoped that this time his film would encourage more young people to join the police. This was not some facile comment. The issue was important enough for the Film Censorship Bill to be passed in 1987 which allowed the censorship of films which corrupted morals and encouraged crime. The first to suffer was Ringo Lam's *School On Fire*.

The absence of politics in Hong Kong film is not because the film-makers are not politically aware. On the contrary, to make films in Hong Kong is to be hyper aware of politics. For example, Taiwan accounted for 20% of ticket sales and would refuse to take release a film if it was shot on mainland China. And in 1983 Tony Leung Kar Fei shot his first film in China, won best actor in the Hong Kong Film

9

Awards, and found it impossible to find an acting job for 2 years. So, film-makers learned to make their political statements through symbolism or by recreating past events and thereby commenting obliquely on current affairs.

With the run-up to the handover of Hong Kong to China in 1997 everybody, and I mean everybody, was careful not to bad-mouth China. Although the Tiananmen Square massacre in 1989 was a great shock to the populace, in Hong Kong no one dared talk about it.

As for filming in China - that brings its own problems. When filming is complete, the authorities confiscate all the negatives. They decide what footage passes their strict anti-political and pornography laws. Then they only allow about 2 hours of film to leave the country. Stanley Kwan once smuggled out footage and was banned from filming in China for 2 years.

On the run up to the handover on July 31 1997 some film-makers (John Woo, Tsui Hark, Ringo Lam) strengthened their links to Hollywood (perhaps as a possible escape route?), others moved to Taiwan and other movie-making centres (Japan, Thailand, Australia), whilst the rest remained (Wong Kar-Wai). It seems that Shanghai, the old movie capital of South East Asia, may become the capital again.

First Shot: Tsui Hark

Hong Kong cinema has learned many things from Hollywood. The whole martial arts boom of the late 60s and early 70s sprang from Robert Wise shooting *The Sand Pebbles* in Hong Kong in 1966 - the local stuntmen saw how Hollywood stuntmen arranged fight scenes, Wise used Panavision cameras which stayed in Hong Kong, locals who worked on the film as assistants started their own film companies.

However, genre film-making in Hong Kong changed when a film maker called Tsui Hark stopped making rather extreme, personal and dangerous films, and started working in the mainstream. Tsui, a graduate of the University of Texas' film school, combined a love of traditional Chinese stories and Western cutting edge techniques, beginning with his directorial debut *The Butterfly Murders* (1979), a flop which has grown in stature over the years. He hit pay dirt with the furiously-paced *Zu: Warriors From The Magic Mountain* (1982), which used an American special effects crew and led to the formation of the first Hong Kong special effects house. He set a certain style, which involved hyper action scenes, fast plot construction, rapid cutting, iconic use of very well known stars, and a mixture of the humorous and the serious, or shocking, elements.

Then Tsui was responsible for rehabilitating John Woo, personally and professionally - Woo's career was in extremely bad shape when Tsui backed him by producing *A Better Tomorrow* (1986), the first sequel (1987) and *The Killer* (1989). Their relationship soured and there remains a gulf between them. (The dialogue between the two central characters in *The Killer* is reputedly derived from Woo's relationship with Tsui.)

Since then Tsui's career has concentrated on more traditional/historical/magical kung-fu fare, continuing the genre he began with *Zu: Warriors From The Magic Mountain*. He has produced the *A Chinese Ghost Story* series, and directed/produced most of the *Once Upon A Time In China* series. More recently, he has begun directing films in America beginning with the Jean-Claude Van Damme actioners *Double Team* (1997) and *Knock Off* (1998).

Tsui deserves a place in Hong Kong cinema history because of his influence on directors, producers, actors and genres, but he has only occasionally directed Heroic Bloodshed movies.

Second Shot: John Woo

Although Kirk Wong's *The Club* (1980) and Johnny Mak's *The Long Arm Of The Law* (1984) are about Hong Kong crime and criminals, they deal with the characters and situations in a realistic way. The innovation that John Woo introduced to Hong Kong cinema is his portrayal of the heroic anti-hero, the chivalrous killer with his code of honour. He adapted the traditional stories of the lone swordsman dealing with problems of honour and face, and transposed them to the modern world, made the hero a triad, and added a surreal kinetic energy. His outrageous visual flair first came to the notice of Hong Kong cinemagoers with *A Better Tomorrow* (1986).

Woo strung together a series of glossy, action-packed films and it was *The Killer* (1989) which broke the Western market, becoming something of a cult hit. Eventually, his reputation got him a foot in the Hollywood door with the Jean-Claude Van Damme starrer *Hard Target*, which was followed by *Broken Arrow* and *Face/Off*. Woo is now a part of the Hollywood establishment. A John Woo interview/article is featured in this Pocket Essential.

Bullet-Point: Names - In Hong Kong, the surname comes before the first name, therefore Tsui Hark is known as Hark or Mr Tsui. By the

11

way, his name is pronounced 'Choy Hok.' Many Hong Kongers have adopted Western names to make it easier for us. For example Wu Yu Sen has become John Woo.

Third Shot: Ringo Lam

Hong Kong cinema is not big on politics. Any criticism of the government, or comment on past events, is censored or almost rigorously ignored by the public. To get your point of view across in a movie you have to be oblique, symbolic. This is how John Woo talked about his politics in *Bullet In The Head* (they stayed away). Ringo Lam has less patience.

Continuing in the tradition of Kirk Wong, who bases his work on real events e.g. *Crime Story* (1993), Lam has provoked much controversy and gnashing of teeth. However, his versatility and skill as a film maker has resulted in some very watchable films like *City On Fire* (1986) - filmed at the same time as John Woo's breakthrough movie *A Better Tomorrow* - and *Wild Search* (1989). Lam's talent lies in showing the grey areas of his characters - people can be both good and evil at the same time. Lam then places these people in an explosive political context - in prison, in school, in the police - and then lets the fireworks go off. He never forgets that people like to watch films with guns, blood, action, stunts and drama.

Dogged by censorship and money troubles, Lam was unable to build a series of successful crowd-pleasing films. After completing a Jean-Claude Van Damme film, *Maximum Risk*, it looked as though Lam was taking the Woo route into Hollywood. However, this was not to be, and Lam remains in Hong Kong making Heroic Bloodshed his specialty. A Ringo Lam article is featured in this Pocket Essential.

Bullet-Point: Kings Of Cantopop - The four major Cantonese singers are also among the biggest film stars. They are Jacky Cheung (*Bullet In The Head*), Andy Lau (*The Adventurers*), Lai Ming (*Fallen Angels*) and Leslie Cheung (*A Better Tomorrow*). Bizarrely, unlike Western pop stars, when given the opportunity they can actually act.

Fourth Shot: Wong Kar-Wai

Although the Hong Kong films of John Woo are in the mainstream, they do not always make money and are not always critically successful. Some, like *Bullet In The Head*, have found better audience response in the West than in their country of origin.

Conversely, although Ringo Lam is a mainstream director, he has received little acknowledgment of his talent in Hong Kong, and even less in the West. In fact, if it was not for Quentin Tarantino borrowing the last 15 minutes of *City Of Fire* for *Reservoir Dogs*, it is doubtful that we would even have heard of Ringo Lam.

This interdependence between East and West is all part of Hong Kong culture. It is a culture which reproduces products for profit. Just as you can find all your favourite designer labels in Hong Kong, you are likely to find all you your favourite movies. *Witness* (1985) became *Wild Search* (1988). *Top Gun* (1986) became *Proud And Confident* (1988) but transposed to a police SWAT squad. *Nikita* (1990) became *Black Cat* (1991).

When John Woo and his contemporaries began to make hit movies, they were not only copied by local film-makers (*Hard-Boiled 2* is not an authorised sequel), but American directors also began to take notice. *Reservoir Dogs* I have mentioned, but *Joshua Tree* (1993) also has a direct swipe (a scene from *Hard-Boiled*). Hollywood eventually decided to swipe the style and talent wholesale which is why *The Big Hit*, *The Corrupter* and *The Replacement Killers* were made in America instead of Hong Kong.

The Heroic Bloodshed style and content seem to have stagnated. Where will the new ideas come from? My guess is the independent cinema, which has brought us the talents of Ann Hui (*Boat People* (1982)), Stanley Kwan (*Rouge* (1987)) and Clara Law (*Autumn Moon* (1992)) among others, will determine the future direction of Hong Kong cinema.

The leader of the pack is Wong Kar-Wai. He steers away from the image of Hong Kong cinema as a purely generic cinema, of martial arts and gangster movies, although he is canny enough to include elements of them in his films to secure financing. He is rather exceptional because, instead of taking his cue from America, he is more in tune with the French New Wave, Japanese cinema, and disparate film and literary sources. The voiceover in *Chungking Express*, for example, is lifted fairly blatantly from hip Japanese novelist Haruki Murakami.

Together with his cinematographer, Australian Christopher Doyle, Wong Kar-Wai has been defining how Hong Kong cinema sees itself. Consequently, the 'smudge-motion' effect used in *Chungking Express*, and the wide-angle lens in *Fallen Angels*, have turned up in many subsequent Heroic Bloodshed movies. A Wong Kar-Wai/Christopher Doyle interview is featured in this Pocket Essential.

Bullet-Point: Subtitles - The original Hong Kong release of a film is normally spoken in Cantonese with both Mandarin and English subtitles. Cantonese is the main dialect of Southern China and Hong Kong. Many earlier films were shot in Mandarin, the official dialect of Mainland China which is also spoken in Taiwan. Hong Kong movies are subtitled into English, or Chinglish as they affectionately call the misspellings and bad grammar. These are often terrible and have led to some hilarious lines - for this reason it is often advisable to buy videos with remastered subtitles.

Fifth Shot: Zhang Yimou

It now becomes less meaningful to think of Hong Kong and Chinese cinema as being distinct. Every Zhang Yimou film, with the exception of his first, *Red Sorghum* (1987), has been financed by Taiwan or Hong Kong or both. Films like *Raise The Red Lantern* (1991) and *Shanghai Triad* (1995) are technically Hong Kong films. It is ironic that these films are made entirely on the Chinese mainland, with almost entirely Chinese casts and crews, but they are legally Hong Kong films.

In the past, most of the important Hong Kong movies have been funded directly from Taiwan, through pre-sales, where distributors could be relied upon to cough-up anywhere up to 75% of the budget. Nowadays, if Taiwan is prepared to invest at all, it will only put in one-sixth of the budget; and the reason for that is simply that no one in Taiwan goes to see the movies any more.

In fact, audiences in Hong Kong, Taiwan and China have, on the whole, stopped going to Chinese films. They prefer to see Tom Cruise in *Mission:Impossible*. The Chinese and Hong Kong industry's share of its own domestic box-office is lower at this point than it has been at any time since the mid-60s. This results in something like half the number of films being made as were made 10 years ago. Taiwan only produced 12 films in 1996.

We have probably seen the end of Hong Kong as a prolific producer of genre movies, and what we shall see replacing it is what we can already see in Taiwan, which is the mavericks, the exceptionally motivated and the exceptionally talented continuing to work. So, Wong Kar-Wai, Stanley Kwan and Zhang Yimou will stay on and continue to do what they have always done.

As for the genre directors and actors, they've gone to America to find greater wealth and prestige. They are all doing it now, because it is only now that the West has become open to them. Had the studios been opening their doors to the likes of John Woo in the 70s, during the first kung fu boom, I suspect he would have been over there like a shot. In fact, John Woo settled his family in Texas 20 years ago and, were he able to direct in the States at that time he would definitely have done so, but the offers did not come. Now John Woo, Chow Yun Fat, Jackie Chan and Tsui Hark are all working for Hollywood.

If Hong Kong audiences prefer to see Tom Cruise in *Mission:Impossible* that is fine. Only, in the future, these films will quite often be made by Hong Kong directors. Witness John Woo filming *Mission:Impossible 2* in Australia.

Bullet-Point: Cat III - This is not a sequel. This refers to Category III movies - movies which contain extreme violence and explicit sex. This is not a taboo category, as the 18 certificate is often seen in the UK - film makers often make films specifically for this category. Popular since the early 90s and mostly released straight to video, they are a sure sign that film producers are now desperate for an audience, any audience. There are also Cat II (violence) and Cat I (family) films.

Parting Shot

Over the last 10 years or so, China has become more and more like Hong Kong. The pace of change in China is amongst the most dramatic and startling in the world. Consequently, there is no question of Hong Kong being submitted to some kind of strange Communist way of life when street level China already resembles Hong Kong's.

China has been ostensibly a one party state since 1949 and the image one has of China, as of other Communist states, is one of social conformity and social obedience. The lived reality is something very different: since the Tiananmen Square massacre, the gap between people and government has been enormous and widening all the time. Essentially, China is incredibly anarchic these days, and there is a kind of tacit agreement with the government that as long as there is no public attack of the government, you are pretty much left alone.

The ones who are affected by this are the ones who are campaigning for change in China's political system - the dissidents, and artists who require a public platform for their work. However, people who do not feel the need to address the public in any large number, go about doing their own thing. China now has, for example, enormous gay discos where you will find transvestites dancing on the tables.

In Hong Kong, the Chinese government do not have to worry about any outspoken political views because the Hong Kong media has been censoring itself for years. Also few film-makers, if any, conform to the image of political dissident. No one, it seems, will openly question the legitimacy of the Chinese government.

Since the handover, it is clear that there has been no radical change in filmic output. It is business as usual. And that business demands a barrage of bullets, and rivers of blood.

John Woo: The Rhythm Of Violence
Article by Steve Holland
Interview by Martin Coxhead

A ballet of bullets and blood, *The Killer* instantly shot John Woo to the forefront of action directors whose films have deconstructed our notions of violence in the cinema: Sam Peckinpah (*The Wild Bunch*), Martin Scorsese (*Taxi Driver*, *Mean Streets*), Quentin Tarantino (*Reservoir Dogs*)...

Choreographed and orchestrated like nothing seen in the West before, *The Killer* turned Woo into a celebrity in the UK where his name had previously been known to only a few hardcore fans of Hong Kong cinema. Rumours that his films were taking action movies beyond any limits Hollywood producers ever dared in their wildest NC-17 dream had filtered across the globe through the pages of magazines like *Eastern Heroes* where Woo was treated like a demi-God of destruction, although never quite raised to Godhood as he would later be by *Select* magazine. And once *The Killer* broke through the dam of conservative taste, the torrent was unstoppable: *Hard Boiled* blew screens apart with its relentless double-fisted gunplay, Chow Yun Fat blazing away in slow motion and shot from multiple camera angles to make sure that every metal-jacketed slug hit its intended target - the viewer. Within weeks, *Hard Target* received its retail video release. It was easily the best-looking Jean-Claude Van Damme movie yet committed to film, although Woo's Hollywood debut was neutered by Universal's desperation for an R rating, which they achieved by extensive cutting and draining it of all excess blood. Since then, there has been a steady thud thud thud of Woo films released onto video - *A Better Tomorrow I* and *II*, *Bullet In The Head* - onto the big screen - *Broken Arrow, Face/Off* - and even onto the small screen - *Violent Tradition, Blackjack*. The steady infiltration of more material into the UK by the slow assassin is itself a rhythm of violence.

John Woo was born Wu Yu Sen in 1948 in Guangchou, Canton, China, to a scholarly father, a philosopher, who found life under the Communist regime intolerable. The Woo family escaped to Hong Kong in 1951, but most of their money was spent on medical treatment for John, who was a sickly child. After the big fire of 1953 they became homeless, lived on the streets and then in the slums. In 1954, his father became sick with tuberculosis and spent the next 10 years in hospital. To support the family, his mother worked as a manual labourer on construction sites. They could not afford to send John and his brother to school, so the boys helped in the church. With gangland killings and riots around him, it was a hell from which Woo dreamed of escaping. His mother introduced him to the cinema - Woo became a fan.

"I was always going to the cinema, constantly. It was a very exciting time because the cinemas were showing everything, Western films as well as Chinese. I went to see almost anything they showed. So what I always wanted to do was work in cinema."

An American family sent money through the church, and John went to a Lutheran school for 8 years from 1956. He was so grateful to the American family and to the church, John wanted to repay their kindness by becoming a priest.

In 1964, when Woo was 16, his father died. His father had taught him a lot about philosophy, Chinese culture, about how to live with dignity. Woo, a bit of a rebel, was fascinated by outside cultures: James Dean, Elvis Presley, The Beatles. He regularly missed school to educate himself in libraries, museums, cinemas, watching Truffaut, Antonioni, Bergman, Kurosawa and his favourite, Jean-Pierre Melville, whose *Le Samouraï* starring Alain Delon was the starting point for *The Killer*. Woo stole film books to learn film theory. He discussed film with friends at the offices of *The Chinese Student Weekly*.

Dissatisfied with Hong Kong film, from 1968 he made four or five 8mm and 16mm shorts over 2 years, some of which survive. The following year he joined Cathay Studios as a script supervisor, supplementing his wages by writing film criticism and using the money to finance his experimental films. His interest moved to the new wave of American directors, Sam Peckinpah, Francis Ford Coppola and Stanley Kubrick. In 1969, Woo participated in anti-war protests, going to many demonstrations and rallies. Later in the year, he became a production assistant for Cathay film studios.

"The film business at that time was corrupt! And it was corrupt in two ways. First, it was very difficult to get into the business unless you already knew someone in it. Very difficult. And secondly, it was corrupt because all they made, apart from the kung fu movies, were imitations of Western films. If there was a big hit in the West then the Hong Kong companies would copy it."

In 1971, Woo became an assistant director at Cathay and then moved to Shaw Brothers Studios, where he eventually worked as an assistant director for veteran pioneer of kung fu movies, Chang Cheh - renowned for his smartly dressed, chivalrous heroes and his unrestrained expression of emotion. These are primary influences. Woo worked on many films such as *The Boxer From Shantung* (1972) and *Blood Brothers* (1973, starring Ti Lung).

"They were only turning out classical costume kung fu pictures - many, many of them - and Chang Cheh was the master. It was great to train under him."

Woo graduated to directing his own movies, aged only 26 - most directors got their first shot in their 40s. Also, he was regarded as an intellectual, which was not what was needed. His first film was an independently financed low-budget kung fu actioner originally titled *Farewell Buddy* which, when completed, proved too violent for the Hong Kong censors. It did, however, attract film distributors Golden Harvest who saw in Woo a talent to be nurtured. He was signed up on a 3 year contract, reshooting scenes of his first movie for release (in 1975) as *Young Dragons*. Next was *The Dragon Tamers* (1974), starring Ji Han Jae, shot in Korea where film-making was cheap and the Koreans welcomed the money spent by relatively well-off film companies and personnel.

"One of the main stunt guys on *The Young Dragons* and *The Dragon Tamers* was terrific. He had great ideas and was brilliant at movement and action, and that was Jackie Chan, so we made him fight choreographer. On *Hand Of Death*, he was also head of the unit but we rewrote it so that he became the lead. I didn't exactly discover him, but I gave him his first real lead. Now of course we're both working in the States!"

Hand Of Death (1975), another low-budget tale of Shaolin vengeance is only notable for casting the young Jackie Chan, with fight co-ordinated by the legendary Samo Hung, and with Woo himself starring as a Shaolin rebel. It was still nothing more than average chop socky action, although a telling line spoken by Woo - "Friends, you are all brave and loyal men. With your courage and devotion we cannot fail" - seems to pre-empt and summarise many of his cinematic themes of loyalty and friendship which he would return to time and time again.

Woo's most successful film of that period was an opera, *Princess Chang Ping* (1975), and it was escaping the restrictions of the kung fu genre that proved his big break. In 1977 came the comedy *Money Crazy*, a box-office hit which established his directorial talent and which he followed with various other films, ranging from *Follow The Star* (1977) in which a beautiful young actress attracts the attentions of inept kidnappers, to the swordplay of *Last Hurrah For Chivalry* (1978). Splitting from Golden Harvest in 1981, Woo joined the newly formed Cinema City, co-founded by producers Dean Shek and Raymond Wong, and directed two more smash hit comedies *Laughing Times* (1981) and *Plain Jane To The Rescue* (1982).

This was not the best of times for Woo who, wanting to break away from comedy, directed *Sunset Warrior*, a bloody modern-day jungle adventure, his first Heroic Bloodshed movie. It's the tale of a team of mercenaries on a mission to capture a drug lord General. Unexpectedly brutal for a Woo flick, it is aided by a terrific performance from Lam Ching Ying (the lead in the *Mr Vampire* series) as a Vietnamese General with a grudge against the team after he is semi-blinded by their leader.

"It was my first modern action picture and they allowed me mostly to make what I wanted. It had a lot of action but it also had the qualities I wanted in the script. The hero is a family man, and although the heroes are all flawed, they all have real qualities, honour and faith. It's good versus evil again. At the end our hero is redeemed, he has to fight for his redemption. The first draft of the script was much more violent, very, very cruel and had more sex in it. I had to shoot some of the sex to please the producers but otherwise I was left alone. It was good doing some of the action scenes, really big battle scenes. I think it works well, although I haven't seen it for a while. I think it's recognisable as mine - it has all the themes I like to use."

The producers were unhappy with the results, so the film was left on the shelf, to be resurrected in 1987 as *Heroes Shed No Tears* in the wake of the box-office smash, *A Better Tomorrow*. But that was still 3 years away, and after *Sunset Warriors* proved a failure, Woo was sent to Taiwan where he directed two comedies before returning to Hong Kong.

"I was always wanting to make a modern gangster film, always, and there just wasn't the opportunity at Shaw Brothers or Golden Harvest. So eventually I went to Cinema City to work for my friend who was a producer, Tsui Hark, and he allowed me to make *A Better Tomorrow*."

Woo had been influential in getting Tsui Hark a contract with Cinema City and now, with Hark producing, he wrote and directed *A Better Tomorrow* for the company as a warning of things to come, reflecting his fears about escalating crime, triad control and the future of Hong Kong itself when Chinese control returned in July 1997. (The film was actually a remake of *True Colours Of A Hero*, an important 60s film directed by Luke Kong.) The film caused a sensation in Hong Kong and Woo found himself the leader in Hong Kong's latest, gun-powered genre: Heroic Bloodshed.

"The impact of *A Better Tomorrow* was huge. It was the most popular film ever in Hong Kong, ran for months, which is very unusual there. It made huge stars of Chow Yun Fat and Leslie Cheung. I felt vindicated in wanting to make a gangster movie when it was such a big hit."

The irony of *A Better Tomorrow* was that Woo has always hated violence. Its litany was for friendship, fighting for justice, faith and moral spirit. In Chow Yun Fat, Woo found a knight for the modern Hong Kong cinema. Already a popular TV actor, big-screen success had until then eluded him. As triad enforcer Mark Gor (literally 'Brother Mark'), Chow starred alongside kung fu movie veteran Ti Lung, who had starred in many Chang Cheh classics before and during Woo's time as an assistant, and Leslie Cheung, who has since gained a measure of international success in *A Chinese Ghost Story* (1987) and *Farewell My Concubine* (1993). The trio form a brotherhood of blood as Ho (Lung) tries to break away from his gangster past and reform after 3 years of imprisonment before he dooms his younger brother Kit (Cheung), a police officer. Blaming Ho for the death of their father and passed over for promotion because of his family's criminal ties, Kit's determination to bring down the new ganglord Shing threatens to tear him in two.

Woo was fully projecting his own philosophy onto the screen for the first time. In many interviews he has said he believes that good exists even in the worst of men, an extension of his Christian beliefs. Sacrifice plays the central role in most of his modern movies, edged on by the twin spurs of friendship and loyalty. The most cold-blooded assassins - exemplified by Mad Dog in *Hard Boiled* - also have a code of honour which separates them from the kill-crazy punk murderers of most Hollywood potboilers. In *A Better Tomorrow*, the sacrifice was made by Mark, crippled in the revenge killing of Ho's double-crossers, and Ho in deciding to leave Hong Kong, risking his life in one last attempt to bring down Shing and end any threat against his kid brother.

Here too was Woo's first choreographed modern battlefield, the tea-room shootout from which Chow Yun Fat can (this time) only crawl away from. Nowhere else is it so obvious that Woo has taken on the American Western as an influence. And the origin of the Gor look? Long coat from Alain Delon, sunglasses from Ken Takakura, matchstick and two gun stance from Clint Eastwood.

On its release, Woo found that his success was a double-edged sword. To help Dean Shek, whose Cinema City was in trouble, Woo agreed to direct a follow-up from a story by Tsui Hark. *A Better Tomorrow II* reunited the three main players via a little cinema jiggery-pokery since Chow Yun Fat's character had died in the first film.

"Chow had to be in it - he was the main reason for the success. So we invented his identical twin brother, Ken, living in New York, who has to come back to Hong Kong to avenge Mark's death [laughs]. I enjoyed it a lot, and at the end I wanted all the characters dead, but the producers wouldn't let me actually kill them. They're just badly wounded, very badly [laughs]. But it was a success!"

With another box-office smash yet another installment was called for, so, with Hark as director, *A Better Tomorrow III* soon hit the screens, this time shot mostly on location in Vietnam. But the title proved so durable that 1994 saw *A Return To A Better Tomorrow*, unconnected to the other three, directed by the prolific Wong Jing (*City Hunter, God Of Gamblers, Hard Boiled 2*). Woo is uncharacteristically dismissive of these.

"No, I have nothing to do with those. Tsui Hark made the third one with Chow Yun Fat, but I had no input. And *A Return To A Better Tomorrow* is nothing to do with me or Tsui Hark, nothing."

A Better Tomorrow and the sequel also marked the return to the screen of Ti Lung, a successful actor in the karate and gangster films of the late 60s/early 70s, including *Shatter*, one of Hammer Film's Hong

21

Kong films, whose career had been eclipsed. It took a major upturn after Woo's epic tales.

"Actually he's sort of retired now. He was a great actor and he had acted over about two decades. He gave some great performances, but he was a little old style for a young audience. He was a real hero type."

Having established himself in the action line, John Woo's next move was altruistic, co-directing *Just Heroes* with Ng Ma. It's a story of family and gangland revenge which featured a plethora of Hong Kong stars including Danny Lee, Ti Lung and Chow Sing Chi, now a massive star in the Eastern comedy world, here playing a very serious role. Produced for Tsui Hark, the film was actually made for his mentor Chang Cheh, almost as a retirement fund.

"We did that film as a tribute to Chang Cheh and we did it for free. Ng Ma, myself and all the actors, we were working for him because we had learned so much from him."

Just Heroes was also responsible for bringing David Chiang back to the screen. Famed in the 70s as the star of the *One-Armed Swordsman* movies and known in the West as the Eastern lead of Hammer's *The Legend Of The Seven Golden Vampires*.

"David Chiang, oh yes, the Hammer vampire film! He was in television, and now he's directing films in Hong Kong and Vancouver."

Throughout the film there are in-jokes at the expense of *A Better Tomorrow*. The most obvious is at the gory, ballistic climax where one of the characters plants guns in potted plants and vases in the same manner as Chow Yun Fat's Mark character.

Woo's successes should have had studios clamouring for his next, cherished project, but suddenly he found his ambitions stalled. Instead of a short pre-production period leading into a tight shooting schedule as was common with Hong Kong cinema, *The Killer* found itself languishing.

"Actually, *The Killer* didn't get much support from anywhere. When I wanted to make it and I brought up the idea as a homage to Jean-Pierre Melville, people just asked 'who's Jean-Pierre Melville?' When I went to the studio we didn't have Chow Yun Fat, and they thought he was the one to open the movie. We were trying to cast someone else because Chow was so big, and so busy.

"That was all my fault because after *A Better Tomorrow* he became such a huge star he was always busy! So after a year Chow knew my situation. I wanted to make the film so badly and I didn't want to do anything else. Chow found out about my problem so he told the studio he would do my film, just to help me. So then the studio gave us full support.

"When I made the film none of the people involved knew what the film was going to look like. I tried to explain to them that the movie was very romantic, is about a killer with a heart who wants to do something good for somebody, to do something good with his life, and his enemy, the cop, starts to understand the killer. When I told them the style, the director of photography or anyone, they just couldn't get it.

"I made the film with a lot of slow-motion, and someone in the studio cut all the slow-motion and I had to fight to get it back. Then I cut the movie together and everyone went 'Oh! It's so romantic!'"

The Killer surpassed *A Better Tomorrow* in almost every department. Chow Yun Fat is Jeff, an assassin for hire who during a hit accidentally blinds a night club chanteuse, Jenny (Sally Yeh). Having broken his unwritten code of honour, he helps the girl who remains unaware of the nature of Jeff's work; Jeff decides to take on one more contract to pay for an urgently required eye operation and then to quit.

The emotional bonds formed by Jeff and Jenny are nothing to those that form between Jeff and the police officer assigned to track him down, Lee (Danny Lee). They interplay throughout the movie, meeting at Jenny's apartment and even though they're on opposite sides of the law, recognise the codes they each live by even when they have guns pointed at each other. The two are thrown together further when Jeff's final assignment becomes a double-cross; a long-time friend of Jeff's is involved and Woo almost hammers home his message that dishonouring a friend is the lowest a man can crawl. The friend is at least allowed to make up for his heinous crime later in the movie.

The finale here is set in an abandoned church to which Jeff heads whenever he seeks a little seclusion. Under a blanket of white doves who nest in the eves, Jeff and Lee honourably face their final showdown with an army of triad killers.

The emphasis on the male bonding partly came about because Sally Yeh, who played Jenny, gave a limited amount of time to the project, being more concerned about her singing career and going on dates with her boyfriend. The original concept of the film was triangular, as later seen in *Once A Thief*. The weakness of his female characters is something which concerns Woo, who has since discussed projects with Sharon Stone and Sigourney Weaver.

In *The Killer* John Woo achieved his first real international success, the film becoming a cult favourite in the USA where it played to art house audiences, a foundation from which further releases were made. Woo's reputation as the doyen of duels and duality grew rapidly, particularly amongst fellow directors like Martin Scorsese, Walter Hill and Sam Raimi, who all publicly acknowledged Woo's standing as an action director. A smaller following began to grow in the UK where Woo's films were notably absent at a time when the kick-boxing craze began to sweep video stores. In fact, it wasn't until the release of *Hard Boiled* in 1994 that Woo gained his first widespread cinema release there.

The success of *The Killer* made it an obvious candidate for that new trend - the American remake. Signed by Columbia Pictures the project was originally to shoot in Hong Kong with Woo directing and Richard Gere and Denzel Washington taking the Chow and Lee roles respectively. It is doubtful the film will ever be remade.

After a small role in the romantic comedy *Starry Is The Night* in 1989, Woo made his most autobiographical and emotionally charged film to date - *Bullet In The Head*. It's the story of three friends (Tony Leung, Jacky Cheung and Simon Yam) whose relationship, built on the streets of Hong Kong, is destroyed by events in Saigon when greed overcomes loyalty. Woo soon found that distributors were unhappy to handle such a long but compelling film, resulting in much of the climatic final reel being deleted. The complete version ran 2 hours 30 minutes.

"The studio were not happy and they took out 11 minutes, and the distributors then cut it further. The Hong Kong version was about 1 hour 45 minutes, something like that. They just showed it without the ending. I was so upset because I made that movie with a lot of pain and heart. It didn't do very well at the box-office. I wasn't understood.

"*Bullet In The Head* was based on two things. Some of it is my biography and some of it was the Beijing Tiananmen Square massacre. I was using Vietnam as the image of the future Hong Kong, the image of people under siege, under dictatorship. All their values, their loyalty, would be lost and people would hate each other so much they couldn't even trust their own friends. It's going to be a very sad place. So that's why I made the movie. I was ruled by my heart and I was so hurt, so pained - I went crazy during it, like Francis Ford Coppola during *Apocalypse Now* - when *Bullet In The Head* didn't get a good response in Hong Kong. I think the people in Hong Kong understood what I was trying to say, but the massacre still lived in their minds and they just didn't want to face any more tragedy."

What was even more tragic was that this was Woo's first film produced by his own company, Milestone, which he formed with Linda Kuk and Terence Chang, and which would produce all his Hong Kong films.

"After I made the movie some people in the film business asked why I'd spent all that money (it went 3 times over budget) on that kind of rubbish? So when the movie failed and I didn't get any phone calls from anyone, it made me understand it was a cruel business.

"I was very surprised when I heard *Bullet In The Head* got a very good response in the West. In Germany, New York, Great Britain, people really love that movie and that made me feel very touched. I must say that movie and *The Killer* are my favourites - they are so complete. The technique, the choreography, the performances, the cutting. They all work."

After the gruelling saga of *Bullet In The Head*, Woo's next choice of production was in a very different vein. *Once A Thief* is almost a throwback to the comedy caper movies of old (*To Catch A Thief* (1955, dir Alfred Hitchcock), *Topkapi* (1964, dir Jules Dassin), *The Hot Rock* (1972, dir Peter Yates)), with Chow Yun Fat, Leslie Cheung and Carrie Cheung as a trio of jewel thieves, dodging hi-tech defences and nabbing gems in the South of France and Hong Kong. The finished product wasn't to Woo's satisfaction and the original *Casablanca*-like ending was reshot. Veering towards comedy and without any explicit violence, but with a thrilling car chase engineered by the French master of motor mayhem Rémy Julienne, *Once A Thief* was a deliberate change of direction.

"At that time the world thought I was a very pessimistic guy but I just wanted to show to the world that I was actually an optimistic guy. I always think there's hope and beauty in the world."

Although only a moderate hit at the box-office, *Once A Thief* was taken as the basis for a TV pilot with the aim of expanding it into a series. Directed by Woo and with the Oriental stars replaced by Westerners Sandrine Holt, Ivan Sergei and Nicholas Lea, it is available on video as *Violent Tradition*. He is honest about his reason for accepting the challenge of a remake.

"So many people thought I only made big movies like *Broken Arrow* or *Hard Boiled*, but there were 2 reasons for doing it. About 1995 a production company, Alliance, and the writers approached me with the idea that *Once A Thief* could be a very popular series. I read the script and saw a lot of interesting things in it. They really got the style right with the romance, and the love triangle, as well as the adventure style and the humour. In the meantime, I was already fed up with the Hollywood system. On every movie I've made there are so many problems, it's so complicated. There's so much going on, so many politics, so many egos. I spent too much time on meetings, I kept changing scripts and I waited too long. I wanted to try something really simple like I did when I worked in Hong Kong. Just concentrate on making a movie, nothing else, and Alliance gave me that opportunity with *Violent Tradition*."

1992 saw Woo make the movie that would catapult him to fame in the Occidental world, and totally redefine the action movie in the meanwhile - *Hard Boiled*. With leading man Chow Yun Fat playing a renegade police officer on the trail of crazed gangster and gun-runner Anthony Wong, while never quite knowing whose side assassin Tony Leung is on - is he an undercover cop or a man playing both sides against the middle? - Woo had all the plot elements for an epic. Beginning with a ballistic shoot-out in a tea-house, the pace rarely slows, aided by intriguing characters and intricate plotting. Spot Woo's cameo as the owner of a jazz club. *Hard Boiled*'s amazing set-pieces culminate in a staggering 25 minute shoot-out in the hospital where Wong has stored his armaments. As opposed to a usual Hong Kong film, *Hard Boiled* had the benefit of an extended shooting schedule.

"It was 123 days. The budget was $4.5 million, US dollars. For a Hong Kong film that's pretty good. We were fully in control of the film so I just kept shooting and shooting and shooting. We were also shooting the film without a script for most of the time. Barry Wong (the writer) died halfway during the film and it was such a pity. He was writing while we were shooting so for half the movie we had no script, we created everything on the set. The hospital set-piece took about six weeks to film, all night shooting, all on actual locations. It was very large scale. The last scene in the hospital was the last scene to be filmed and we were shooting nearly 36 hours straight. We had to because it already had a cinema date planned and the company was waiting to release it.

"I wanted also to do a little experiment with it. I wanted to make the action scenes like a war movie, very energetic. I don't like using hand-held camera. I prefer to use a dolly or a track, to have everything steady, keep the movement smooth. In Hollywood I sometimes use Stedicam but I'm not really in favour of hand-held."

One unusual aspect of *Hard Boiled* was the use of Michael Gibbs, a young British composer, for the soundtrack.

"In *Hard Boiled* I was trying to use a composer from overseas because I thought he would bring something new to the movie. When we found Michael I was so surprised that he would do it because at that time we had no money left! Just no budget for the composer! But he didn't mind. He just wanted to work on the film for very little money. The other thing was that we only gave him a rough-cut tape which ran over 2 hours. We gave him the tape and just asked him to put something to it. He did a fantastic job with the music. It really brought up the movie, and I was so ashamed that we couldn't pay him enough! I really appreciate his work on *Hard Boiled*."

The gunfights were more ballistic than ever, the set pieces more explosive, as summed up by Woo when he described the final showdown between an army of gun-running triad soldiers and the police force at the triad base, hidden in a hospital. Escaping with a baby tucked under his jacket, Chow Yun Fat was clearly in pain.

"In the final sequence Chow is holding a dummy baby and there are about 7 big explosions behind him. On the first take I had him running in slow motion towards the camera...on the first take I wasn't satisfied because he almost ran off camera. I said 'It was the wrong timing, it was too late.' The special effects guy said that if it blew up too soon Chow could get hurt and he wouldn't do the stunt. So I said, 'Okay, so we won't tell him!' We ran it again only this time the explosions were much quicker and Chow starts running scared and his hair got burned at the back."

The first thing Chow asked after the shot was "How did it look?"

All this violence from John Woo, a man who failed karate and has never fired a gun in his life. Woo, influenced by the musicals he watched as a child, choreographs the gunshots when he edits, making music from them. Even though he films his characters reloading, these scenes are often left on the cutting-room floor because inserting them disrupts the rhythm.

Hard Boiled sealed Woo's international reputation and Hollywood beckoned, offering *Hard Target* starring Jean-Claude Van Damme. (Actually, Woo wanted Kurt Russell, who was unavailable, so he was given Van Damme.)

"There were a lot of offers before *Hard Target*. I had so many Hollywood scripts, and most of them were nothing, just action, action, action. I wanted a new experience. Then they sent me the script of *Hard Target* and the original script was pretty good, good characters. Then the producers, the writer and Jean-Claude Van Damme flew to Hong Kong to see me. They asked me to do the movie and when we met I said I really wanted to give it a try - I believed I could make Van Damme's breakthrough as a star. I had done it with Chow Yun Fat and Leslie Cheung, and I thought I could do it with Van Damme. But he wanted changes in the script and I thought I could deal with that. Also, I liked the producers (Sam Raimi and Robert Tapert, creators of *The Evil Dead*).

"For Hong Kong companies there is always limits - you can really only do action or comedy. If you want to try something about politics, or the government you find it very hard, they make it difficult to shoot. I've made action and comedy for over 25 years and I needed a change. In Hollywood there are so many talented writers and so many studios I thought I would get more choice of projects. My dream was always to make movies in different countries. So Hollywood is not my only ambition. I wish I could make a film in London, or Ireland, or Greece, Germany, anywhere. I want to meet different people and learn from different cultures."

Hard Target showed little of the interplay that Woo's own stories contained. A straight thriller, it was based around the premise of *The Most Dangerous Game*, the hunting of men for sport, with both stars - Jean-Claude Van Damme and Lance Henriksen - putting in sterling performances. But to reduce the rating from NC-17 to R, Woo's cut was leached of blood by Universal and the ratings board, the dreaded MPAA. Whilst it packed a punch, it was hardly the showcase he would have liked.

"There was a movement at the time towards less violence on television, and that spilled over into film. I think my name caused some tension, made the ratings board keep an eye on my film! They made us re-cut the film 7 times, and they would never let us know what was the real problem. So we have to cut the film by guessing - we never knew. 20 gunshots? Cut it to 15 perhaps? Cut it, always cut it. Then the board would just say cut it again! It was so rude! I was so mad, but you just need to compromise with the MPAA. I didn't mind cutting it if they would only let us know what the problem was."

Kinetic action and chase scenes aside, *Hard Target* also had a great villain in the shape of Lance Henriksen.

"Lance is a great actor and he's a good friend. Actually he's also an artist, he paints, he sculpts, plays the piano. He built his house with his own hands. He's so artistic. He makes everything himself. He's actually playing the piano in *Hard Target*. He's got a kind of gift, anything he wants to he can learn."

The future for John Woo seemed clearly mapped out: *Shadow War* was to be his first American cop movie, this time a male and female facing terrorists, and a two-film deal with Fox was to bring *Tears Of The Sun* and *Ring Of Blood* to the screens, the latter developed by Quentin Tarantino was poised to launch Chow Yun Fat on a Hollywood career. However, the transition was not to be so simple - Woo dropped out of both projects. Instead, he formed a company, WCG Entertainment, with Terence Chang and Christopher Godsick, and directed *Broken Arrow*.

Broken Arrow by *Speed* screenwriter Graham Yost was, as American TV host Jay Leno observed, probably the first film in which two nuclear bombs are hi-jacked and one actually goes off! When the weapon detonates, having been hidden in an underground mine by Stealth Bomber pilot turned bad guy John Travolta, the entire Utah desert ripples through the underground shock wave, a dazzling scene created by CGI (Computer Generated Imaging). It's a system with which John Woo is impressed.

"When I read that in the script I wondered just how we were going to do it. Then I saw the test footage the animators had done digitally and it was perfect! I realised that we could do anything the script demanded."

But, to carry out all these special effects, stunts, image processing etc. requires detailed storyboarding and preparation before any film is exposed. This is a long way away from filming on the streets of Hong Kong, making it up as they went along like, for example, on *Hard Boiled*.

Woo's inspiration for *Broken Arrow* was Alfred Hitchcock's *North*

By Northwest, probably the definitive man-on-the-run movie. He wanted every moment, from first to last, to be full on excitement, intensity, energy, humour. And that's exactly what Woo delivers.

Then Woo delivered *Face/Off*, a SF thriller starring John Travolta as an undercover cop who joins the mob by altering his appearance to that of his nemesis. It's about good and evil, two men switching their identities, their lives entwined, interchangeable. Released in the summer of 1997, it rocked, to put it mildly.

Talk of collaborations with Martin Scorsese (*Dirty Boulevard*) and Quentin Tarantino fill the occasional column in magazines. Woo himself has said he would like do a remake of Jean-Pierre Melville's *Second Breath*, and his dream is to make a historic movie in mainland China, *The Romance Of The Three Kingdoms*, based on a famous civil war that took place 3000 years ago. With the people of China, Taiwan and Hong Kong not getting along to put it mildly, this epic would be a metaphor for today's situation and a reminder that they must give up their hatred for each other. More recently, Tom Cruise and Paramount eyed Woo as a possible director for *The Devil Soldier*, a biopic (based on a 1992 book by Caleb Carr) of mercenary Frederick Townsend Ward who was taken to China in the 1850s by the Emperor to quell the Taiping rebellion during the 12 year civil war that killed 20 million people.

While waiting for his next big film to surface, Woo found time to direct another TV movie, *Blackjack* starring Dolph Lundgren as a detective who has a fear of the colour white. Cue scene of Blackjack in a room filling up with milk!

Having relocated his family to America, it's obvious that Woo recognises the new Hong Kong/China has no place for him. A director in demand, Woo has affirmed his stature as a Hollywood director by being offered *Mission:Impossible 2*. Filmed in Australia, starring Tom Cruise it is set for release in the summer of 2000. After that, he films *Knight's Gambit* with Chow Yun Fat.

John Woo has taken Heroic Bloodshed far beyond anyone's expectations. Woo may now dance to a different drummer, but the beat remains the same.

Heroic Bloodshed Filmography
Reviews by John Ashbrook (JA), John Costello (JC),
Paul Duncan (PD).

A Better Tomorrow (1986)

Literal Chinese Title: *True Colours Of A Hero*

Dir: John Woo. Cast: Chow Yun Fat, Ti Lung, Leslie Cheung, Emily Chu, Lee Chi Hung.

Chow Yun Fat plays Mark Gor, wearing a long black overcoat, Ray-Bans, and chewing a toothpick. He is just so cool. It broke all Hong Kong box office records. Surprisingly, Chow's casting was controversial at the time because, although well known for his TV work, he'd never made a particularly successful film up until then.

The central character is Mark's partner Ho (Ti Lung), who wants to give up the triad life because he doesn't want to stand in the way of his younger brother Kit (Leslie Cheung), an ambitious cop. After a sensational shootout, Mark is crippled, Ho goes to jail, and Kit is devastated when he finds out his brother is a gangster. Years later, when Ho gets out of jail and wants to go straight, the triads just won't let him alone. Realising he has to end it once and for all, Ho gathers his friends for the showdown to end all showdowns. Epic.

105m, Widescreen, Subtitles, (The collectors box set contains a booklet, original trailer, filmed interviews with John Woo, Chow Yun Fat and Ti Lung) MIA, 18, ☆☆☆☆ PD

A Better Tomorrow II (1987)

Dir: John Woo. Cast: Chow Yun Fat, Ti Lung, Leslie Cheung, Dean Shek.

Chow Yun Fat returns to play Ken Gor, long lost twin brother of Mark Gor, who is out to avenge Mark's death. Enormously bloody shootout at the end. As one might suspect, this is not as good as the first one.

100m, Widescreen, Subtitles, Made In Hong Kong, 18, ☆☆☆ PD

Just Heroes (1987)

Dir: John Woo, Ng Ma. Cast: David Chiang, Danny Lee, Chow Sing Chi.

John Woo directed about 60% of this conventional crime movie.

It was made to raise money so that veteran movie director Chang Cheh could retire in comfort. The story reflects this sentiment, being about young gangsters coming to terms with the murder of their revered uncle. There are lots of crosses and double-crosses, action set pieces and points of honour as the guilty party is revealed. (It also has one of the funniest closing lines I've come across in a movie - "Do you still want to be a Boss? Or do you want to run a fish business?")

Nothing special, but still worth watching for the sly references to *A Better Tomorrow*.

93m, Widescreen, Remastered Subtitles, MIA, 18, ★★★ PD

Heroes Shed No Tears (1987)

Dir: John Woo. Cast: Eddy Ko, Lam Ching Ying, Chen Yue Sang, Lau Chau Sang.

Originally filmed in 1983 as *Sunset Warrior*, this film sat in storage until John Woo hit it big with *A Better Tomorrow*. Up until this point Woo had mostly directed comedy, so this was a sort of test run for his Heroic Bloodshed movies.

You know what's wrong with spaghetti westerns - the shocking 'acting', laughable 'scripts' and appalling dubbing (not, to be fair, that there is any such thing as 'non-appalling dubbing'). Well, all of those things are also wrong with *Heroes Shed No Tears*. However, in common, also, with Sergio Leone and the like, this film rises above its countless inadequacies to show a director and a genre that, although still teething, demonstrate genuine and considerable promise.

Captain Kirk (yes, really) leads a gang of mercenaries through The Golden Triangle, battling drug-lords and dictators wherever he finds them (i.e. around every corner). This turns into a vendetta when Kirk's opposite number, having lost an eye due to him, wages a single minded war against him and his troops. It's really just a feeble excuse to string together ever-more ambitious and gruelling fight sequences. Some of the stunts are extraordinary, given the shoe-string budget, and some of the violence positively sickening, particularly a sequence where the bad-man-with-no-name sews Kirk's eyes up.

Character development? Sub-plots? Acting? A Jedi craves not these things!

A hotch-potch of *Dirty Dozen*, *Southern Comfort* and *Apocalypse Now*, this film unpretentiously forms part of a bridge between the rural empty-hand epics of the early 70s, and the urban gangster noir of the late 80s. As such, it is an uncomfortable experiment, but of considerable curiosity value to Woo watchers.

And that title's a blatant lie. At the end; beaten, torn, hacked, shot and grieving his fallen comrades, Kirk does find time to squeeze out a small tear. The big jessie. You never see Chow Yun Fat blubbering over spilled blood.

85m, Widescreen, MIA, 18, ★★★ JA

The Killer

Literal Chinese Title: *Two Blood-Splattering Heroes*
Dir: John Woo. Cast: Chow Yun Fat, Sally Yeh, Danny Lee.

This film has always left a slightly sour taste in my mouth. Whilst there's no denying it was here that Woo's jaw-dropping virtuosity with action set-pieces finally reached the peak it has yet to tumble from; I've never been entirely convinced by the film's morality.

Morality? In Heroic Bloodshed? Has he fallen completely off his trolley?

No, not completely. Normally a Woo film strives to make sense of mankind's violent impulses, usually deciding they are as utterly self-defeating as they are inevitable.

Problem is, *The Killer* purports to actually give a damn about the innocent bystanders who inevitably get it in the neck during these epic shoot-outs. Anyone who's watched any number of HB movies, knows that 'collateral damage' is as big a harvester of Hong Kong's innocent-passers-by as lung-cancer and road-accidents combined. So, when brutal hitman Chow's muzzle-flash blinds a woman, he is so chewed-up with remorse, he decides to arrange for her to have sight-saving surgery. And how does he propose to pay for this heroic act? By gunning down another poor, unsuspecting sap. Obviously the phrase 'two wrongs don't make a right' must lose something in the translation to Cantonese.

Visually, the film breaks with HB tradition in that it employs a lot of Christian imagery. Of course, this is philosophically meaningless to Buddhists but, I suspect, Woo includes it because, if nothing else, the crucifix is symbolic of the sacrifice and martyrdom he wishes on his lead characters; whilst the Madonna they so-spectacularly blow-up, stands for Chow's guilt.

So, ignore the 'redemption through extreme violence' nonsense, and just enjoy John Woo, the Choreographer General, firing on all cylinders ... and both barrels.

107m, Widescreen, Subtitled, Made In Hong Kong, 18 ★★★★ JA

Bullet In The Head (1990)

Literal Chinese Title: *Blood In The Streets*

Dir: John Woo. Cast: Tony Leung, Jacky Cheung, Waise Lee, Simon Yam.

John Woo is one of the Grand Masters of pumped-up, rollercoaster action movies working in cinema. He learned his craft making low-budget exploitation thrillers in Hong Kong. He became a Name after the success of his outrageously fast 'n' furious flicks *Hard Boiled* and *The Killer*. He became a Player when he took his act to Hollywood and made a decent Van Damme movie (*Hard Target*) and utilised the Travolta phenomenon to go stratospheric with *Broken Arrow*. This may have been his master plan all along, as on the evidence of this belatedly-released 1990 feast of mayhem, all he ever wanted was...to be American!

Imitation is the sincerest form of flattery, and *Bullet In the Head* is John Woo's tribute to American movies (quite a few of them make guest appearances, and there's a whole sequence lifted from *The Deer Hunter*), a buddy-movie with Epic pretensions which ultimately fails because he forgot to include the ponderous bits. For example: while there is a Wedding Scene, it only lasts for a couple of minutes; small fry next to Cimino or Coppola who can be relied upon to spin weddings out for at least 20. However, if it fails as Epic it sure as hell succeeds as Entertainment.

Ben (Leung, excellent), Frank (Cheung) and Paul (Lee) are the best of mates in the turbulent climate of Hong Kong circa 1967. Anti-colonial demonstrations are brutally stomped by the authorities, poverty and unemployment are on the rise. The three do everything together - drink, chase skirt, rumble. All for one and one for all.

On Ben's wedding day there is a shortage of cash to pay for the reception, so Frank borrows from the local loanshark. On his way back he is jumped by small-time hood Ringo and his gang, but retains the cash at the expense of a beating. When retribution is exacted, the first of many tragedies ensues: Ben accidentally kills Ringo. The three find themselves on the lam in Saigon with suitcases packed with pills to sell. The action continues at an incredible pace: a suicide bomber takes out their taxi and their suitcases. They fall in and then out with a major-league crime boss. Finding an ally in his disaffected henchman Luke, they steal his cache of gold and his squeeze. They are pursued by the Vietcong, captured and forced to kill other prisoners. Friendship is the major casualty as greed and survival instincts take over. The final conflict is played out 3 years later in Hong Kong, mano a mano of course.

Woo's trademark dissolves, freeze-frames and slow-motion passages are much in evidence and his set-pieces, be they battles or urban fisticuffs, are superbly shot and choreographed. The dialogue however rarely rises above trite exposition ("One day I'll come back in a Mercedes," "With guns in our hands, the world will be ours").

Ultimately, this is a movie with its heart pinned to its sleeve. American cultural icons abound and American directors influence is omnipresent. A selection: The Monkees, JFK, Elvis, Sam Peckinpah, Oliver Stone, Michael Cimino, George Lucas.

Bullet In the Head tries too hard to encompass everything for its own good, slewing around insanely as it goes for its shots, but it is undeniably exhilarating stuff and should satisfy fans and the curious alike.

126m, Widescreen, Remastered Subtitles, Made In Hong Kong, 18, N (originality) ★★★★ (style) ★★★★★ (big-time explosions & guys with guns) JC

Once A Thief (1991)

Literal Chinese Title: *Criss Cross Over Four Seas*

Dir: John Woo Cast: Chow Yun Fat, Leslie Cheung, Cherie Cheung.

This is one of the slightest of John Woo's films. Even so, it stands head and shoulders above the rest of the straight-to-video market. Although it stars Woo's lucky-charm, Chow Yun Fat, it wears quite a different guise from any of the other films they have made together - it's an unashamed comedy.

Taking inspiration from the fount of all heist movies Jules Dassin's *Du Rififi Chez Les Hommes* (aka *Rififi*, 1955) and *Topkapi* (1964) with maybe just a hint of Hitchcock's *To Catch A Thief* (1955), this is a breezy and brash high-speed heist movie.

Even though the presentation may be totally different, the regular Woo concerns of group-loyalty over minor concerns such as legality, are here for all to see. In flashback we are introduced to Chow and his 2 adopted sibling's abusive guardian - the mastermind of their early crimes, and, by contrast, the benevolent policeman/uncle who rescues them from the gutter. Later, their dilemma becomes a struggle between these two forces as their ex-guardian wants them dead whilst their ex-uncle is the inspector in charge of bringing them to justice.

The set-pieces are crafted with the usual Chinese precision, the stunts being no less demanding of the actors and stunt-performers than in the more serious movies. Where this film scores is in the shoot-outs, which are text-book demonstrations on how to empty a clip without actually hitting anyone. The body-count is low, the violence skillfully skirted round and, consequently, this is a great way for the young and uninitiated to get into Hong Kong action cinema.

104m, Widescreen, Remastered Subtitles, Made In Hong Kong, 15, ★★★ (by Woo standards) ★★★★ (by everyone else's) JA

Hard Boiled (1992)

Literal Chinese Title: *Ruthless Supercop*

Dir: John Woo. Cast: Chow Yun Fat, Tony Leung, Teresa Mo.

Sergeant 'Tequila' Yuen (Hong Kong heartthrob Chow Yun Fat) is a *Dirty Harry*-type maverick cop whose overdeveloped sense of justice invariably lands him in trouble. After losing his partner in a hail of triad bullets, he wages an unauthorised guerrilla campaign against arms-dealing crime boss Johnny Wong. In doing so, he clashes repeatedly with Wong's cool, mysterious henchman-for-hire Tony (Leung, again excellent) who has switched allegiance to Wong after despatching former boss Mr Hoi and his men, and presenting Wong with Hoi's weapons cache. Wong views Tony as a protégé but his chief gunman Mad Dog isn't so sure.

When encoded messages appear in flowers sent to Yuen's ex-girlfriend 'madam' Teresa (Mo) warning him off Wong's case, Yuen begins to suspect the presence of another. After a further encounter where Tony has him cold but spares his life, Yuen realises he has found his undercover 'partner.' The two form an uneasy alliance based on grudging respect and set out to discover the whereabouts of Wong's arsenal. Tony's cover is blown and the *Die Hard*-inspired climax takes place in a hospital owned by Wong, the basement of which not only houses a morgue but the weapons stronghold. The race is on to get the patients out before Wong's men detonate explosives all around the hospital.

Hard Boiled has little depth. Almost zero character development. A Frankenstein monster of a plot with bits of American thrillers stitched together in a haphazard tapestry of mayhem. Little time for diversions down paths of plausibility or logic. Scant regard for notions of good taste.

Hard Boiled is my favourite John Woo movie.

John Woo doesn't care much for social realism or narrative structure. He does care about crafting turbocharged variations on the Hollywood gangster/thriller formula and has the audacity to throw in a whole boxful of new tricks too. Therein lies the secret of his popularity and his assimilation into the US studio machine.

This quietly-spoken, unassuming man is the Count of Body-Count, the Auteur of Disorder, the Magus of Chaos. Nobody does it better.

I love John Woo's films in much the same way as Sergio Leone's or Luc Besson's. These people do not believe that directors should hide behind their material, that they should remain anonymous. They believe in calling attention to their style, however shallow that may appear to some critics.

Hard Boiled may also have a parallel to be drawn with Italian giallomeister Dario Argento in its reliance on astonishingly staged set-pieces to propel the movie forward. Or perhaps I should say jet-propel, because this film moves along at a tremendous Tasmanian Devil's pace. The editing is lightning fast and full of flourishes like wipes, slo-mo, freeze-frames, dissolves and multiple combinations thereof. The camera is a prowling beast, stalking the action: following, passing, towering above, worshipping from below, zooming in, pulling back. And then there are the lenses: fish-eye, wide-angle, the lot. There's more action and invention in 10 minutes of *Hard Boiled* than in the whole of a James Bond movie. It is a precisely choreographed bullet ballet with technical virtuosity and panache to spare.

At over 2 hours, the film is packed with images that stay with you, and two set-pieces in particular are worth the entrance/rental fee alone. The first, a shootout in a crowded tea-room, is so dazzlingly brilliant that it's almost impossible not to rewind and rewatch if you're in front of your TV and VCR. The second is in a larger, more open space, but is no less impressive: Wong's men ambush Hoi's operation in a warehouse, using motorbikes and machine guns, and are then in turn ambushed by Yuen who achieves mythical levels of destruction.

In Yuen, John Woo has given us a hero, a hybrid of comic book and movie character who is triumphant in every situation to the point of indestructibility. Movie audiences traditionally respond to heroes of this calibre. Where Takeshi Kitano provides thoughtful, angst-ridden characters doomed to suffer at the hands of fate, John Woo gives us a sure-footed superman who lives to fight, and win, another day.

Me, I just sit there enjoying the hell out of it, grinning and shaking my head.

122m, Widescreen, Remastered Subtitles, (special edition includes 60m of John Woo interview and clips) Tartan, 18, ★★★★★ JC

Hard Target (1993)

Dir: John Woo. Cast: Jean-Claude Van Damme, Lance Henriksen, Wilford Brimley.

Hard Target begins in the dark and dangerous streets of New Orleans, a man is pursued, hunted by an organised gang. Their job? To stop him in his tracks and take from him the money belt strapped around his waist. It is an urban fox-hunt, with an unarmed down-and-out ex-soldier as the fox and the pampered high-velocity rich as the hounds. Already we can witness the fluid editing, the slo-mo detailing and the sheer gutsy drive of a John Woo fillum. Vigilant viewers will also notice that the sell-through video (labelled as the 'full uncut version') actually contains a considerable amount of material not previously seen even at the cinema. Cumulatively, the extra shots amount to no more than a minute, and they were obviously removed for the sake of pacing, not censorship, but it is still interesting to see what was, in effect, a work in progress.

When originally released, a certain amount of criticism was levelled at this movie for stealing its hunter-and-hunted premise from Ernest B Schoedstack's *The Most Dangerous Game* (1932). Personally, in a movie environment where *Mon Père Ce Héros* can take twelve months to turn into *My Father The Hero*, I think Woo can be forgiven for pinching from a 60-year-old movie.

Temporarily leaving the side of his usual leading man Chow Yun Fat, Mr Woo took up with Jean-Claude Van Damme. He plays Chance Boutreau, a homeless, penniless Cajun with a nice line in kick-boxing and rescuing endangered damsels. He displays the thick strain of nobility which marks out a Wooian goodguy from the usual all-smoking, all-swearing chaff and, as with everyone else in the movie, is less a character, more an archetype.

Cue Lance Henriksen as the mad-eyed organiser of these urban hunts. Woo experiments with ways of seeing this character and, in a remarkable scene devoid of dialogue, shows Henriksen hammering out a ferocious piece on a snow white grand piano whilst glaring fixedly at his own reflection - this moment speaks volumes. As is so often the case, the villain is a far more interesting piece of work than the hero, and Henriksen lets rip in a way that not even *Near Dark* led us to expect.

The film soon boils down to a straight conflict between Henriksen and his cronies on one side, Chance on the other. But this simplicity merely serves to clear the way for Woo's aestheticism to play. There is a pseudo-religious moment when Chance's uncle (played by the ever-irascible Wilford Brimley) hands over a silver shotgun by tossing it in slow-motion through a convenient beam of mote-filled light. It is a fleeting moment given significance by the diligent Woo - the passing of a torch, handing down of a family trait, call it what you will - it bonds the two men in a far more meaningful and imaginative way than the usual heavy-drinking, arm-wrestling kind of male bonding.

Similarly iconic is the moment when Henriksen 'rapes' Natasha, by forcing her to remove a long, hard bullet from his belt-pouch and slide it significantly into the barrel of his gun. It is arguably the most savage act of the movie.

Every line of dialogue, every gesture, every shot has been considered and re-considered for its beauty and for the information it imparts. Woo uses his actors almost as marionettes, placing them very particularly before allowing them to extemporise, and the result is very much 'a John Woo film' rather than just another vehicle for J-CVD. This is a morality tale which, to Woo, is more important than the people involved in the telling. The film's packaging carries a quote from the inimitable Quentin Tarantino, crediting Mr Woo as 'doing for action what Hitchcock did for suspense,' which, given his auteurist control is not an inappropriate comparison. It is also the highest imaginable compliment and I wish I'd thought of it.

97m, CIC Video, 18, ✫✫✫ JA

Broken Arrow (1996)

Dir: John Woo. Cast: John Travolta, Christian Slater, Samantha Mathis, Delroy Lindo, Bob Gunton.

Combine the ruthless narrative of *Speed*, the unashamed pomposity of a Bond film and, naturally, the visual flair of Mr Woo, and you have ... a western.

Well, okay, this version of *Broken Arrow* isn't a western in the traditional sense, but neither is it a John Woo film, in the traditional sense. He practices great self-restraint in employing his trademark stylistic flourishes, and this tale carries very few of the thematic hallmarks we expect from him - no moral ambiguity, no personalities in transformation.

What it has, in spades, is his passion for narrative drive. As befitting a script written by Graham Yost, this story builds up a good head of steam early on, and then ploughs on remorselessly until its inevitable spectacularly destructive conclusion.

But about that western idea – filmed against the evocative mid-western landscapes through which we have grown accustomed to seeing John Wayne ~~mincing~~ striding - this *Broken Arrow* tells the traditional western tale of a conflict between two men, one unquestionably bad, one unquestionably good. Both are cut off from the censure of civilisation. Out there, on the frontier, you make your own rules, and you fight your own battles.

Where this film deviates from the standard cowboy mentality, is in the casting: Travolta is quite obviously having a whale of a time as the badguy, grinning and twitching his way through such wonderfully over-the-top lines as, "Would you mind not shooting at the thermo-nuclear weapon."

Meanwhile, Slater, the good-guy, is too busy running, jumping and not standing still, to get much snappy dialogue. If charisma were a lightbulb, Travolta's would blind you, whilst Slater's would need a new filament. Inevitably, then, you find yourself rooting for the badguy.

I don't know about you, but I really wanted to see Utah go boom; and it is part of the film's mischievous audacity that I actually got my wish, whilst Salt Lake City still made it to the end titles unscathed. Oh well, maybe next time.

104m, Fox, 15, ★★★★ JA

Violent Tradition (1996)

Dir: John Woo. Cast: Sandrine Holt, Ivan Sergei, Nicholas Lea, Michael Wong, Jennifer Dale.

We eagerly awaited John Woo's *Once A Thief: The TV Series*, especially since Woo agreed to direct the pilot episode himself. Inappropriately retitled *Violent Tradition*, there are only the merest vestiges of *Once A Thief* here. Where once we had a binary opposition of good uncle and bad father tugging at the loyalties of three adoptive siblings, we now have a division between the threesome. Where once we had three siblings working together to bring down their father's evil schemes, we now have one brother who supports his father 100% whilst the other two are conscripted into The Agency. Where once we had a good uncle, we now have *The Man From UNCLE*.

Although the reasons for these changes are obvious - a series needs a consistent framework (The Agency) and a nemesis (evil brother Michael) - it is less obvious to me why the humour has drained from the piece. Where once we had good-humoured repartee and wittily conceived heists which evoked the great high-camp heist movies of the past, we now have unfunny one-liners delivered to a stonily unimpressed audience of adversaries. Yet, the heists are presented just as jokingly, when the rest of the movie is played as deadly serious.

Although there are occasional flashes of the Woo magic - such as a scene where two characters tussle over a bunch of roses - they are few and far between. What we have left is a confused plot about dislikeable characters. There is little or no chemistry between the players, making it all seem depressingly like an episode of *Bugs*; indeed, even the characters who sleep together don't actually seem to like each other.

But still, it's a pilot, and pilot episodes are rather like dress rehearsals for plays - if they are a disaster, that's usually a good omen for the series. If you're gonna make mistakes, make 'em early and improve quickly. With *Violent Tradition*, there's plenty of room for improvement.

96m, BMG, 15, ★★ JA

Face/Off (1997)

Dir: John Woo. Cast: John Travolta, Nicolas Cage, Joan Allen, Alessandro Nivola, Dominique Swain, Gina Gershon.

Broken Arrow caused a few raised eyebrows among Woo's long-term fans, and they gave him a real ear-bending for it. However, his third bite at the Hollywood apple was a real about-face for him, allowing him to turn the other cheek to those who said he'd thumbed his nose at them. Taking such criticism on the chin, he put his nose to the grindstone and ... alright, alright, I'll stop.

Given John Travolta's dominance of the mid-90s box-office, he really was the guy no one dares say 'no' to. So, when he decided that he was going to re-team with Mr Woo for the most extreme, preposterous and complicated representation of the action movie aesthetic ever, the bosses at Disney swallowed hard and signed.

Since Woo had turned the action movie into an art form when

Hollywood still thought Schwarzenegger, Stallone and Norris were the Holy Trinity, they shouldn't have feared - their money was in the safest possible hands.

Initially, Nicolas (less is more) Cage gets to chew the furniture, then, at the end of the film's extraordinarily elaborate first act, Travolta returns to form. Two dream roles – both by turns seriously sentimental and surreally psychotic – the sort of roles actors pray for!

Of course, personalities in transformation have long been Woo's fascination, demonstrated most perfectly through his way of turning the audience's sympathy on its head. Here you get to root for the goodguy *and* the badguy, at the same time.

The most perfectly realised Woo moment, the culmination of 25 years at the sharp end of exploring the minds of the violent, comes during the elegiac shoot-out in the hall of mirrors. Travolta and Cage meet face to face to face to face, a sheet of mirrored glass between them, symbolising how, given the proper motivation, the transformative power to harm is within us all.

Face/Off is an electrifying mix of action, metaphor, epic tragedy and science fiction. Wonderful, ludicrous, extraordinary stuff. Stop reading this book and go watch it. Now!

138m, Touchstone, 18, ★★★★★★ JA

BlackJack (1998)

Dir: John Woo. Cast: Dolph Lundgren, Phillip MacKenzie, Kam Heskin, Fred Williamson, Saul Rubinek.

Accustomed to working far harder than his Hollywood contemporaries, John Woo feels the need to fill the gaps between his big-budget extravaganzas with TV movies such as this. Just to keep from getting rusty, like.

Here Dolph Lundgren plays bodyguard-for-hire Jack (who, fairly obviously, isn't black...). In the 15-minute prologue, Jack comes to the aid of an old friend whose daughter is being threatened by gangsters. Cue extensive shoot-out involving flying furniture, heavy ordnance and, of course, a carton of milk and a trampoline.

When I first approached this film, I was concerned that, as with *Violent Tradition* (1996), Woo may have only faxed in his directions. After that scene with the milk-carton and the trampoline, there can be no doubting whose hand steered this ship to shore.

And so, finally, on to the main plot. Jack is called in by another friend to guard a super-model, known as Cinder, who is being hunted by a wide-eyed (and spectacularly inept) psycho who wants to do more than just establish her shoe-size. Jack must protect her from him, from her own suicidal tendencies and, of course, from the incompetent official bodyguards, who seem able to keep everyone from her, except the killer.

The 'gimmick' is that Jack is allergic to the colour white, and goes blind whenever he sees it. A tad inconvenient since the entire film is shot in designer white hotel-rooms, crisp white hospital corridors or grand, echoey ballrooms with billowing white curtains. If only the film had been called 'Whitejack'!

107m, Alliance Communications, 18 ★★ JA

Non Heroic Bloodshed Filmography

The Boxer From Shantung (1972, assistant to Chang Cheh)

Blood Brothers (1973, assistant to Chang Cheh)

Young Dragons (as Wu Yu Sheng, 1973, released in 1975)

The Dragon Tamers (1974)

Princess Chang Ping (1975)

Hand Of Death (as Wu Yu Sheng, aka *Countdown In Kung Fu*, 1975)

Money Crazy (aka *The Pilferer's Progress*, 1977)

Follow The Star (1977)

Hello, Late Homecomers (TV episode, 1978)

Last Hurrah For Chivalry (1978)

From Rags To Riches (1979)

Laughing Times (as Wu Hsiang Fei, 1981)

To Hell With The Devil (1981)

Plain Jane To The Rescue (1982)

The Time You Need A Friend (1984)

Run Tiger Run (1985)

Ringo Lam: In Sheep's Clothing
Article by Paul Duncan

He's a mystery. Here's a guy who's directed a film whose last 15 minutes bear some similarities to *Reservoir Dogs*. He's directed a pile of docudramas, as he calls them, which were heavily censored in the East and are rarely seen in the West. It was about time somebody did some legwork and found out who this mystery man is...

Little Lam

He was born Lam Ling Tung in Hong Kong in 1955. When he was growing up everybody in Hong Kong worshipped Western culture: Elvis Presley, James Dean, that sort of thing. The young Lam went to a party where a girl asked him if he had an English name. He said no. They were dancing to a Beatles tune so she gave him the name Ringo. He only met the girl once but the name stuck.

After graduating from High School in 1972, Lam joined an actors' training class in 1973, where he met Chow Yun Fat - they've been friends ever since. Lam spent one year on the course, which was organised by TVB, Hong Kong's biggest and best TV network, owned by Sir Run Run Shaw. After working six months or so as an actor, he realised he didn't like people pointing their fingers and telling him what to do. He shifted to work behind the camera working as a production assistant until 1976, then as a television director and writer until 1978. Some of his colleagues included Tsui Hark and Ann Hui (*Boat People* (1982)).

Disillusioned with television, Lam moved to Canada for the next three and a half years to study film making at York University in Toronto. In 1981, he returned to Hong Kong without his degree but with Canadian citizenship and started looking for his first movie. After 2 hard years, Karl Maka, the head of Cinema City, offered Lam the job of completing *Esprit D'Amour* (1983). Director Leong Po-chih had already filmed about a third of the script before having a dispute with Karl Maka, and Lam was hungry enough to step in to complete it. A romantic ghost comedy starring Alan Tam (Hong Kong's top pop star at the time) and Ni Shu Chun, it was both critically acclaimed and a smash hit.

Cinema City produced comedies so Ringo Lam directed more comedies: *The Other Side Of A Gentleman* (1983), a romantic comedy starring Alan Tam again, *Cupid One* (1984), a yacht comedy starring singer Sally Yeh and Mark Cheng, and *Aces Go Places IV: Mad Mission* (1985), a high-budget action comedy starring Sam Hui, Karl Maka and Sally Yeh. These films taught Lam how to make movies, but he didn't want to make comedies. He wanted drama.

Sheep

After filming *Aces Go Places IV*, Lam wanted to make a police thriller with a script that emphasised strong characters. Since Lam had made

44

so much money for Cinema City, Karl Maka gave him a budget and the freedom to pick his subject.

Lam read a newspaper story about a jewellery robbery in Tsimshatsui, Kowloon. It was bizarre because the police seemed to know the crime would be committed - the police were swiftly on the scene, greatly outnumbered the robbers and even recorded the crime on video. The whole case was very suspicious, so Lam started looking into the background. He talked to the police, and went to court to see the robbers. The gangsters were very badly dressed and looked like losers. He thought that an undercover cop had infiltrated the gang and set about writing the story. But he did not want to just write a realistic story. He wanted to romanticise the situation, the characters, and cast Chow Yun Fat, the undercover cop, as a tragic hero, a man who will ultimately be a victim of his own feelings. Also, the previous four films Lam had made were not of his choosing. He felt helpless and tried to include that feeling of helplessness in *City On Fire*.

As much as possible, Lam tries to put in his feelings from his own life experiences into his movies. The music score, by Teddy Robin Kwan, is mainly saxophone - when Lam left Toronto to move back to Hong Kong, he left his wife behind. On the trip back, he stopped off at San Francisco, went to Chinatown, and heard a saxophone player in the street. That has always been a lonely sound for Lam, so he asked for it to be in *City On Fire*.

City On Fire (1986) starred Chow Yun Fat and Danny Lee. It was made at the same time as *A Better Tomorrow*, so when both films came out, overnight Chow becomes a heroic, romantic lead character. A box office success, Lam won the best director prize at the Hong Kong film awards, and Chow Yun Fat won best actor.

Can I just say, regarding *Reservoir Dogs* being the last 15 minutes of *City On Fire* - there are obvious similarities, but both films are heavily influenced by a long history of crime and western movies. For example, the sliced time structure of *Reservoir Dogs* comes from *The Killing* or, more precisely, the source novel *Clean Break* by Lionel White. There is no major plagiarism of *City On Fire* - they are different movies. Lam, for his part, says that all films learn from each other and, if it was not for *Reservoir Dogs* then there is a good chance that people in the West would not have heard about *City On Fire*.

So Ringo Lam had found his niche: the docudrama. Although not documentary, his street scenes feel like real life, teeming with people going about their business. The fights do not look choreographed - they are chaotic, accidental, with people confused shooting their own people. There is no rhythm to the violence. The characters must make hard decisions where there are no good outcomes. Things happen to Lam's characters. They are not heroes. There are no easy resolutions.

Wolf

Lam continued telling stories about characters who are not in control of their own destiny.

Next was *Prison On Fire*, based on the real-life experiences of Lam's friend Nam Yin. He told Lam many stories about prison life: how the prisoners have their unit leaders, how one time a triad leader called a hunger strike, the gang fights, how one survives in prison. In a locker, Nam found a note: 'Endure, and the sea is calm; retreat, and the sky is wide.' Using that expression as the starting point for the characters and plot, and adding Lam's strong feeling of brotherhood towards his friend Nam, the result was *Prison On Fire*.

Nam Yin had never been a scriptwriter before. He finished a draft for *Prison On Fire* in 7 days. It was a good script with lots of details, but the plot line was weak. Lam gave him some suggestions, about how to arrange the material and to tighten it up and, after a rewrite, it was ready as a shooting script. Shooting took about 20 days. To keep the film as near to reality as possible, Nam Yin was present throughout to make sure that the details were correct and faithfully rendered.

Actors and others behind the scenes often regard Ringo Lam as a demonic presence on the set. He is intense, single-minded. He finds shooting painful because it is not easy to get the stuff he wants - he is only collecting the raw material. His favourite part of film-making is the editing, because that is when he starts to tell the story, where he can control what happens.

Prison On Fire (1987) starred Chow Yun Fat and Tony Leung, and was a box office hit throughout South East Asia.

The Film Censorship Bill passed in 1987 allowed the censorship of films which corrupted morals and encouraged crime. The first film to suffer at the hands of the censorship board was Ringo Lam's *School On Fire* (1988). Starring Sarah Lee and Cheung Yiu Yeung, it depicted a kind of *Blackboard Jungle* in the schools of the New Territories. To save the film from being banned outright, Lam and his producer literally went down on their knees and begged. The result was the release of the film with 36 cuts. It had even more cuts for the Taiwanese market. Worse, it was banned in Singapore and Malaysia,

Having bared his teeth to the ultra-conservative, ultra-sensitive South East Asia market, they stayed away in their millions, afraid of the big, bad wolf. Lam had to make sure he stayed in a job and stayed working.

Sheepish

Fed up with the way people kept censoring his work, Lam went around looking for films he did not have to get too involved with, so that it was not painful when they were censored. He got scriptwriters to write screenplays, then just filmed them.

Wild Search (1989) is an unashamed remake of Peter Weir's *Witness*, starring Chow Yun Fat and Cherie Cheung in the Harrison Ford and Kelly McGillis roles. Chow Yun Fat is far better in many ways in Lam's films. He is less comic-book, more like a normal person. His gentleness, passivity, the feminine side of him comes across because he does not have to spend all his screen time with macho posturing. *Wild Search* is romantic, human, has meaningful action, realistic dialogue - no wonder lots of people liked it around the world.

Undeclared War (1990). Scripted in two weeks, with a US $3 million budget, shot in sync-sound, on three continents in English, Cantonese, Mandarin, and Polish, this international production bombed in South East Asia. It starred Olivia Hussey, Peter Lapis and Danny Lee in a terrorist story, not based on true events, that did not sell. Lam misjudged what he thought a Western audience wanted - he put lots of non-stop action in it without putting in the human interest/interaction a Western audience expects.

Touch And Go (1991). Although Lam directed this, and added a realistic edge, consider it a film in the style of its star, Samo Hung (leading actor, director, fight choreographer). The film broke even, but did not perform as well as expected.

Lam does not like doing sequels (his own *Prison Of Fire* spawned many rip-offs which flooded the market) but he needed the money, hence *Prison on Fire 2* (1992). Starring Chow Yun Fat and Chan Yung-Sung, it was a different situation to the first film. Its pre-sales put it into profit - not on Lam's rep, but because Chow was attached to the project. This put Lam in an awkward position - if Chow had a suggestion, then it was likely to be included, mainly because Lam did not want to argue with his friend. The final cut still proved problematical - 20-25 minutes was cut before it could be released.

There is a tradition in Hong Kong that, if you want to raise funds, you make a film and give the profits to a deserving cause. Everyone gives of their time for free. *Twin Dragons* (1992) was conceived to raise funds to build the headquarters for the Hong Kong Directors Guild. Starring Jackie Chan, and co-directed by Tsui Hark and Ringo Lam, the film did not perform well enough for the Directors Guild to get their new headquarters.

Lam's career in the 90s has not been helped by a comment he made about the Tiananmen Square Massacre of July 4 1989. After 2 weeks of mourning in Hong Kong, Lam had got fed up with all the wailing and gnashing of teeth so, on TV, he said, "Can we have a break for a while? Let's have the Dragon Boat Festival." The backlash against him was so bad he had to spend a month in hiding in Singapore. He received threats, and has since found it difficult to get good reviews in Hong Kong.

So after a few rough patches, it was about time Lam tried something different.

The Slaughter

Up until now, Lam's films have always treated violence realistically. There are a couple of wild moments, confusion, stray bullets - it is not orchestrated. He does not compromise. People are caught in the system, and the system is at fault.

One of the *On Fire* films had 40 cuts and in Taiwan can only be shown in a 60 minute version. Lam realised he was getting too close to reality. Since *Prison On Fire*, whenever his films come out, many responsible people are sent to watch them: officers, lawyers, educators from schools. If one of them thinks his films are too real, that they might not be suitable for public viewing, perhaps they would ban him altogether? Lam wanted to make films that would not be cut, so he stopped making the *On Fire* films.

I suspect Lam had seen David Lynch's *Wild At Heart* (1990) and thought 'neat.' His next film, *Full Contact*, is very stylised and cinematically self-conscious, unreal. Normally, Lam has naturally lit streets, shot almost in a hand-held documentary style. In *Full Contact*, everything seems so dream-like, unreal, drenched in colour. Every place is a set, decorated and constructed specifically for the scene and context. Even the colour - instead of his naturalistic high-contrast bleached colour, Lam used deeper richer colours. Completely different to his *On Fire* series.

During the shooting in Bangkok there was lots of arguing between the crew members, with everybody complaining about each other. Friend was against friend when they should have been working in harmony to make the film. This inspired Lam to focus the film on the theme of friends betraying friends.

Full Contact (1992), starring Chow Yun Fat, Ann Bridgewater, Anthony Wong and Simon Yam, goes further than any other Hong Kong actioner - more heroic, more bloodshed. Ironically, there is more gore and blood and violence in this film than in his *On Fire* films but, because it is not rooted in everyday reality, the censors found it acceptable. In fact, it was too violent for the Hong Kong public, but has been very well received in Japan and the West.

Next was *Burning Paradise* (aka *Rape Of The Red Temple*) (1994), an all-out kung fu actioner, a remake of Joseph Koo's *Blazing Temple*. It did bad business in Hong Kong but again is well-liked in the West.

The Adventurers (1995) started life as a story given to Lam by director/producer Wong Jing (*God Of Gamblers*, *Naked Killer*). Lam did not mind because he brings his personal feelings and ideas to stories which change them, make them his.

Whereas John Woo's major theme is duality and friendship - all his films have the same basic elements told and explored in different ways - Lam has different voices, different people, different subjects. In *The Adventurers* (an inappropriate title) one man wants revenge for his father's betrayal and murder and, to do this, he must betray and murder. This revenge is not a cathartic release for his pain, but a painful responsibility which costs him dearly: the lives of his friends and lovers.

There is character development/change and it is done with integrity and humanity. Lam's characters make hard decisions where there are no easy, clear-cut solutions. People are hurt, die, there is no way out. Violent acts are ultimately desperate and painful, rather than sheer action hero bravura. The resolution rests upon the emotions which drive the film, not the action itself. At the end, instead of greeting cheering crowds and a kiss from the romantic interest, Lam's characters receive a heightened understanding of their world and their place within it, as a result of their actions.

Grey Fox

It is the 'greyness' to his characters - people who are neither good nor bad but trapped - which is the essence of a Lam movie.

Lam was visiting his parents in Toronto after finishing *The Adventurers* when he got a phone call offering him a Jean-Claude Van Damme movie. Although Lam had heard horror stories about John Woo's experiences filming *Hard Target*, Lam was happy to direct a Hollywood movie.

While filming and editing together *Maximum Risk* (1996), Lam was given complete freedom by the studio. Central to the movie was the idea that the audience should not know if Natasha Henstridge's character was for or against Jean-Claude. This, Lam thought, would create tension and ambivalence. However, when it came to previewing the film, the audience gave Natasha bad marks. The studio interpreted this to mean that the audience did not like her, and Lam did 3 days of further filming to change her character. As a result, Lam does not consider *Maximum Risk* to be his movie because the meaning had been changed.

Although Lam added a realistic edge, *Maximum Risk* is a film in the style of its star, Jean-Claude Van Damme. This is not a bad movie, but it is not a Lam movie. Consider it a foot in the door, like John Woo's *Hard Target*.

So far that foot has only been a toe. Lam has co-produced *Simon Sez* (1999) in Hollywood but all of his subsequent directorial output has been Hong Kong-based: *Full Alert* (1997), *The Suspect* (1998) and *Victim* (1999). Like many of Lam's films, they remain largely unseen and unknown in the West.

Although Lam may be trying to enter Hollywood in Woo's clothing, do not let it pull the wool over your eyes. Lam is a thriller director, not an action one, and is more concerned with showing people as they really are, rather than their fantasy alter egos. It is a shame he is still lurking in the shadows, rather than in the limelight he deserves.

Heroic Bloodshed Filmography
Reviews by John Ashbrook (JA), Colin Odell & Michelle Le Blanc (C&M).

City On Fire (1986)

Dir: Ringo Lam. Cast: Chow Yun Fat, Danny Lee, Sun Yueh, Roy Cheung, Carrie Ng.

City On Fire lays down many of the motifs later Hong Kong action movies would emulate. Its concerns are those of violent men, trying to maintain a spirit of brotherhood-under-fire in a teeming, crime-choked metropolis. As it becomes increasingly difficult to tell the gangsters from the police, who can we turn to for help? No one. We have to help ourselves by - as the saying goes - any means necessary!

Chow Yun Fat is a disgraced and disgruntled cop, who has been so far under cover for so long there's almost no one left who knows he carries a badge. He even forgets himself occasionally. He makes contact with the local bad guys, and persuades them that he is a gun-runner will equip them for their next bank heist. Unfortunately, so deep under cover is he, the police also believe he is a gun-runner.

Since this film inspired *Reservoir Dogs*, you may be forgiven for thinking that it doesn't sound very similar. You're right, it doesn't. That comes with the last 15 minutes or so where Lam whips up a hectic, messy and pessimistic rendering of the tale Quentin Tarantino presented in a far more leisurely fashion 4 years later.

Ranging in styles from the slickly noirish to the cluttered documentary style of the New Wave, *City On Fire* is a film which ultimately suffers from its own ambition. This film could have easily been expanded into a trilogy but Lam obviously wanted to make something that was hectic and instant and reflected the million stories available in the naked peninsula.

101m, Widescreen, Remastered Subtitles, Made In Hong Kong ★★★★ JA

Prison On Fire (1987)

Dir: Ringo Lam. Cast: Chow Yun Fat, Tony Leung, Tommy Wong, Roy Cheung.

Lo Ka Yia (Tony Leung), in prison for an accidental killing, is befriended by tough but lovable Mad Dog (Chow Yun Fat), who teaches him the ropes. However, prison guard Boss Hung (Roy Cheung) constantly agitates the inmates and trouble ensues. Tense and understated, there are still plenty of fight scenes to satisfy the bloodshed quotient.

School On Fire (1988)

Dir: Ringo Lam. Cast: Fennie Yuen Kit-Ying, Roy Cheung Yiu-Yeung, Damian Lau Chung-Yun.

A schoolgirl witnesses a triad crime, reports it to the police, and goes through hell as a result. The violence is so extreme that it is unlikely to be released in the UK.

Wild Search (1988, 18)

Dir: Ringo Lam. Cast: Chow Yun Fat, Cherie Cheung.

Ka-Ka is a little girl, about fourish, who is the only witness/survivor when her gun-runner mother is murdered by her clients. Only she can identify Uncle Bullet and bring him to justice. Chow Yun Fat, in charge of the case, finds himself taking responsibility for the child (who calls him Uncle Mew-Mew) and returns her to the rural community from whence she came. Once there, he meets and falls for Aunt Chei (Cherie Cheung), and so has to juggle professional responsibility with personal involvement.

The set-up is clearly and unashamedly Peter Weir's *Witness*. It also uses culture clash to generate moments of comedy, pathos, romance and drama. Where director Ringo Lam deviates from straight plagiarism is that this is less a remake, more a reinterpretation. Lam uses some of the same motifs and plot devices as *Witness* but seems to employ them as inspiration to get him past the blank page stage. Once the ball is rolling, he lets it go where it likes.

As with all of Lam's Hong Kong films, there's a lot going on here, with several plot threads tangling around Mew's feet. He has a hard time keeping his superiors off his back, as he does tracking down the evil-doers, whilst trying to maintain a relationship with Chei and Ka-Ka, and then there's the small matter of Chei's ex. Also, typically, when the violence does burst onto the scene, it is a messier, more visceral violence than you find in, say, the classic Woo films, more dependent on physical contact than big guns.

It seems a shame that Lam's films get overlooked in the frenzy to worship at the feet of John Woo because, although his style is different, it is as particular and as confidently handled as any you will find.

99m, Widescreen, Remastered Subtitles, Made In Hong Kong ★★★★ JA

Undeclared War (1990)

Dir: Ringo Lam. Cast: Danny Lee, Tommy Wong, Olivia Hussey, Vernon Welles, Rosamund Kwan, David Heddison, Peter Liapus.

International terrorists, led by Welles and Hussy, murder the family of a US Ambassador in Poland. Liapus, brother-in law to Ambassador Heddison and a CIA to boot, tracks the terrorists to Hong Kong. He is paired with cop Danny Lee, and they try to stop Welles disrupting a big business conference.

Prison on Fire 2 (1991)

Dir: Ringo Lam. Cast: Chow Yun Fat, Yu Li, Tommy Wong, Roy Cheung.

Boisterous Chow Yun Fat tries to keep peace between HK and mainlander prison factions, but ends up being set up for murder and a revenge hit. The evil warden nearly combusts when Chow and his mainlander buddy escape, resulting in a series of improbable (though invigorating) chases. It's a sombre melodrama with a hilarious twist at the end (that is, if you've seen the original *Prison On Fire*). Like *School On Fire*, this is unlikely to be seen in the UK because of the extreme violence.

Full Contact (1992)

Dir: Ringo Lam. Cast: Chow Yun Fat, Simon Yam, Anthony Wong, Bonnie Fu.

Ringo Lam's finest film defies conventional analysis with its delirious barrage of images and pop art sensibilities. Crafting his colour palette almost entirely from neon, the comic book aesthetics perfectly match the extremities of all the major characters. And what characters they are. Simon Yam is gloriously camp as heistmeister Judge, resplendent in snakeskin jacket and with an astonishing, showy cigarette lighting technique. Virgin is anything but, sexually charged to the point of psychosis, her beefcake boyfriend Deano is so stupid it's amazing he can even breathe. Jeff, our hero, is constantly saving his weak brother Sam from loan sharks, his bouncing skills enhanced by some showy butterfly knife work. Teaming with Judge's gang for 'just one job' to get Sam the money he owes, Jeff is betrayed and spends time recovering in Thailand before returning to enact a calculated and bitter revenge.

What sets *Full Contact* head and shoulders above the competition is its uncompromising and showy technique. Rain splatters off Jeff's gleaming knife. Clubs throb with trashy glitterballs and pounding strobes. Jeff sitting astride a huge motorbike, lurid graffiti in the background, beats Arnie in *T2* any day. And then there's the outrageous sequence from the bullet's point of view that is the most astonishing since *Performance*. The car stunts. The heist. The innocent passers-by embroiled in the mayhem. Simon Yam - awesome, psychedelic and utterly unlike anything you've ever seen. Surprisingly this was not a hit in Hong Kong, it was too excessive. We loved it.

92min (cut 34 secs), Widescreen, Subtitled, Made In Hong Kong, 18 ☆☆☆☆☆ C&M

Burning Paradise (1993)

Dir: Ringo Lam. Cast: Lee Tien San, Wong Kam Kong, Carman Lee.

Not bloodshed but with plenty of blood shed, *Burning Paradise* is the unlikely twin to Lam's *Full Contact* in its denial of realism and grand operatic execution. Like its more famous twin, this is a film of stylistic excess and bold brushstroked characters, with the intensity dial turned up to 11. Combining electrifying new wave martial arts action (Tsui Hark produced, although occasionally the film feels more like a humourless *Last Hero In China*) with a soupçon of wuxia thrown in, the pacing never fails to engage. Fong Sai Yuk, his sifu murdered, is captured with runaway prostitute Tou-Tou and taken to the Red Lotus Temple - a Boschian Hell of burning red and umber, where the passing of time is noted by the decaying arm of a half buried corpse. Releasing the multitude of slaves from the trap-laden temple is not going to be an easy task, especially when the abbot, Kung, is a nihilistic psychopath with a total disregard for any life. Wong Kam Kong steals the show as the wild eyed, mad artist Kung, killing ally or foe without regret and gleefully wrenching the head off of an unfortunate girl, because he wants to! Unfortunately Lee Tien San cannot begin to compete with this performance. Deranged even by Hong Kong standards, the unforgivingly cynical tone, the gratuitous violence, high production values and incredible wirework make this an acquired taste. Breathtaking but too much for some, *Burning Paradise* was another box office disaster for Lam.

95mins, (aka *Rape Of The Red Temple*) Widescreen, Subtitled, MIHK, 18 ☆☆☆☆ C&M

The Adventurers (1995)

Dir: Ringo Lam. Cast: Andy Lau, Ng Sin Lin, Rosamund Kwan, Paul Chun Pui, David Chiang.

Ringo Lam's film is a huge, riotous joy compared to the restrained fumbling of *Maximum Risk*. As is the convention with recent Hong

Kong movies, its locations range all over, from Thailand to San Francisco, in a laudable attempt to display a cosmopolitan sensibility which Hollywood isn't capable of.

As with *City On Fire* and *Wild Search*, it chomps through set-ups and genres like they're going out of fashion (which, it turns out, they were). Yet, at heart, it is a simple revenge tragedy:

Yan has a twenty year-old blood debt to pay. His Cambodian parents were slaughtered by billionaire politico, Ray Lui. As the film begins, Yan and friend Mark, both fighter pilots in the Thai airforce, coldly orchestrate a clever, but disastrous, assassination attempt on Lui, which plunges all involved into an elaborate tale of espionage, violence, kidnapping, and marriage (!) whilst a simple blood-lust unravels into a plot to depose a dictator, free a country and destroy a massive gun-running operation.

In between the shoot-outs and car-chases (all of which are handled with the matter-of-fact brilliance that Hong Kongers make seem so easy), humour and genuine pathos are never far away. Having escaped certain death 3 or 4 times, Yan and his soon-to-be-wife Crystal find themselves walking through wilderness towards San Francisco's distant lights. Lightning dances through the clouds overhead and Crystal observes that Heaven must be taking pictures of them.

Eventually, all things being circular, the plot threads re-entangle in the jungles of Cambodia, where an exhilarating and worryingly large-scale showdown involves helicopters swooping out of the sun and a tree line disappearing beneath the flare of a napalm burst.

I love the smell of sushi in the morning!

110 mins, Eastern Heroes ★★★★ JA

Maximum Risk (1996)

Dir: Ringo Lam. Cast: Jean-Claude Van Damme, Natasha Henstridge.

For all his faults, Jean-Claude Van Damme can certainly pick directors. Having revived the career of Peter Hyams and introduced John Woo to the States, he then headlined Ringo Lam's first foray into La-La Land.

Jean-Claude really is the workhorse of the Hollywood action scene, churning one out every 6 months, regular as clockwork; each one timed carefully to avoid competition and earn him at least one week atop the box-office chart. I suppose it's a formula that works, so why change it?!

As a piece of formulated film-making, *Maximum Risk* is neither as diverting nor as different as *Hard Target* was. It doesn't really stand out from the action movie mainstream, which is a shame given that Lam is the spiritual father of *Reservoir Dogs*, and therefore partially responsible for the renaissance in Hollywood shoot-'em-ups.

The very promising opening sequence features J-C VD dying a nasty death. Cut to local cop, also played by ol' J-C, who discovers that the corpse is actually that of the brother he never knew he had. Determined to find out how and why his brother wound-up cold on the mortician's slab, J-C assumes his brother's identity and takes his return flight to New York.

Precedent would indicate that a new eye on the New York skyline can make it look alien and new. Not so with Ringo; he completely fails to exploit the similarities between New York and Hong Kong. Curiously, he is much more at home in the low-rise vistas of Nice.

The film's middle-act is a leaden bore, plodding from one lumpen chase to the next. However, there are moments to hint, teasingly, at what might have been - the fight in the sauna, played-out to the accompaniment of an accordion, is the highlight of the New York story. The film comes alive again when the production moves back to France for a showdown which is masterfully handled and sparkling with all the energy and imagination of a great Hong Konger.

Unfortunately, these great set-pieces are too few and far between, being separated by a tedious array of moments like the one when J-C and new girlfriend (inherited compassionately from his ex-brother), whilst being held hostage, manage to distract their captor's attention long enough for a quickie against the bathroom door. Yeah, right.

95 mins, Columbia Tri-Star, ★★ JA

Full Alert (1997)
Dir: Ringo Lam. Cast: Ching Wan Lau, Francis Ng, Blackie Ko, Amanda Lee.

Police Inspector Pao (Ching Wan Lau) is assigned to find an architect's killer, and discovers the murderer is former engineer Mak Kwan (Francis Ng). At Mak's home the police team discover weapons, explosives, and safe designs, which leads Pao to believe Mak is planning a major robbery. Mak refuses to talk about the plan. Meanwhile Mak's girlfriend Hung has secretly contacted Mak's Taiwan gang who engineer a prison escape. A game of cat-and-mouse ensues, only this game involves car chases, gun battles and, eventually, the Hong Kong

Jockey Club. The action is punctuated by well-written and well-acted drama scenes (as with the best Lam movies), and the themes of duality and the guilt of violent men are shown through the characters of Pao and Mak. To some a remake of *Heat*. To others a return to the vibrancy of Hong Kong action cinema pre-handover.

The Suspect (1998)

Literal Chinese Title: *Extreme Serious Criminal*

Dir: Ringo Lam. Cast: Louis Koo, Julian Cheung, Simon Yam, Ray Lui, Ada Choi, Eric Mo.

Although the title and poster makes this look like a rip-off of *The Usual Suspects*, it is only similar because it is about a search for a criminal mastermind. Don Lee (Koo) spent 12 years in prison for the murder of an important person. Upon his release, he is asked to kill a Presidential candidate but he fails - his former partner Max Mak (Cheung) does it instead. Now everybody suspects Don of the killing and he must hunt down the mastermind behind the scheme to prove his innocence.

Victim (1999)

Dir: Ringo Lam. Cast: Ching Wan Lau, Amy Kwok, Tony Leung Ka Fai.

Manson (Ching Wan Lau) and his wife Fu (Amy Kwok) are unemployed and running out of money when Manson is kipnapped and beaten by a gang. Fu and Police Inspector Pit (Tony Leung) locate Manson in a house and, over time, find him behaving out of character.

Pit and his team think that Manson has been possessed by a ghost - 30 years before there was a horrible murder in the house where he was found. However, when they go back to the house, they find more than they expected... Horror? Comedy? Heroic Bloodshed? Lam keeps his cards close to his chest - you have to watch the movie to find out what it is about.

Non Heroic Bloodshed Filmography

Esprit D'Amour (1983)

The Other Side Of A Gentleman (1983)

Cupid One (1984)

Aces Go Places IV: Mad Mission (1985)

Touch And Go (1991)

Twin Dragons (1992) co-director with Tsui Hark

Wong Kar-Wai & Christopher Doyle: Available Light
Article & Interviews by John Ashbrook

Wong Kar-Wai was born in Shanghai in 1958, but moved to Hong Kong when his parents relocated there in 1962. His memories of this period form the backdrop to *Days Of Being Wild* (1991) the film that first brought him together with cameraman Christopher Doyle, and got him noticed in the UK.

During the mid-80s he worked in Hong Kong script factories, turning out ten produced scripts between 1982 and 1987, ranging in style from romantic comedies to Hong Kong's trademark action dramas. Promoted to director, he made his first movie in 1988 - *As Tears Go By*. Modelled on Scorsese's *Mean Streets*, it tells the story of two gangland debt-collectors in Kowloon, who look upon each other as brothers. Little brother Fly's constant posturing to prove that he's a man means that Big brother Ah Wah, is forever bailing him out. Eventually the resentment between different 'families' within the gang come to a head in a brutal torture scene which, in typical Hong Kong fashion, manages to be as nasty as it is stylish.

All the motifs which would become Wong's calling card are here - love-lorn loners, a claustrophobic urban jungle, lit in strongly contrasting shades of red and blue, a popular music background, sudden explosions of extreme violence shot in a time-distorted blur now known as 'smudge motion.' Similarly, his leading man Andy Lau, in common with many Hong Kong stars (including Jackie Cheung who played Fly), is not just an actor but also a million-selling recording artist and movie producer. Wong loves taking huge celebrities and presenting them as average, every day people. Of course, this aspect is rather lost on us here, where most people haven't heard of any of 'em. It is worth remembering, however, that both Lau and Cheung won Best Actor awards for their performances in *As Tears Go By*.

Wong's next two films *Days Of Being Wild* and *Ashes Of Time* (1994) were something of a departure, being respectively a historical romance and a martial arts epic.

Days Of Being Wild tells the story of a disappointed and debauched young man, Yuddi, whose life seems meaningless to him because he doesn't know whom his parents are. Women fall at his feet and he does nothing more than abuse them, not caring for anyone who has the bad taste to care for him. As with *As Tears Go By*, this tale is about a person's need for family, and what the cost of that can be. It features Wong's first use of voice-over and multiple story lines, which he uses to jump from perspective to perspective, and from location to location, usually without warning.

This is a much calmer film than its predecessor, allowing its historical setting (1960) to show a peaceful and uncluttered side of Hong Kong which is ignored by the action movie mainstream. Indeed, it isn't until the story relocates to the Philippines that Yuddi encounters any gangsters.

Ashes Of Time became the crucible in which Wong Kar-Wai's film-making concerns were burnt down to the very basics. In this elaborate two-year production, he and Chris Doyle learned once and for all what they didn't like about Hong Kong cinema. It remains unreleased in the UK.

Chris Doyle is Australian, although at the age of 18, somewhere in the early 70s, he left Sydney to join the Norwegian Navy - presumably because a Norwegian ship was the first one to come along. After that he pursued various 'career options' including selling quack medicine in Thailand and digging wells in the Indian desert, before being 'reincarnated' by a poetry and language teacher at the Hong Kong University in the late 70s. She gave him his now notorious pseudonym Du Kefong, under which he still directs the occasional movie.

As well as running theatre workshops, publishing books of his behind-the-scenes photographs, producing television documentaries and creating collages, Doyle directs pop videos for the stars of the movies he works on ... oh, and in his spare time he is Chinese cinema's most in-demand director of photography.

After their exhausting experience on *Ashes Of Time*, Wong and Doyle decided to do something completely different, something fast and cheap and improvisational: they made *Chungking Express* (1994). This film and its sort-of sequel *Fallen Angels* (1995) bring together everything that Wong had been experimenting with: a huge cast of dysfunctional characters; several plots; lots of voice-over; sudden punches of violence (to keep the distributors happy) shot in that trademark 'smudge motion' style; claustrophobia; glaring artificial light; and Doyle's energetic hand-held camerawork.

The end result is as emotional as it is exhausting. It is a

quantum leap away from the mainstream action movies of John Woo and the like, whilst bearing all the artistic and stylistic hallmarks that Hong Kong films uniquely bring with them.

Their next film, *Happy Together* (1997), bore no resemblance to anything that came before. The story of two gay Chinese lovers in Buenos Aires, it has served to endear Wong Kar-Wai to the art house crowd even more, if that is possible. Their next two films *Beijing Summer* and *2046* are due for release in 2000.

The following interviews took place just before Wong Kar-Wai and Chris Doyle departed for Buenos Aires to film *Happy Together*.

Wong Kar-Wai

I was late for my interview with Wong Kar-Wai. Something to do with a miscalculation about the time difference between Britain and Hong Kong. I was exactly one hour late. Nevertheless, Mr Wong was still sitting in his office, waiting for me to call. He mentioned that I was late, but didn't seem to mind. In fact, he found my inability to add 7 to 12 quite amusing. He finds many things amusing. This unnerved me a little - he's supposed to be a serious artist whose films are highly regarded and have won him many fans and many awards around the festival circuit. He's the respectable face of Hong Kong action cinema. He can't have a sense of humour as well, surely!?

He talks calmly and quite slowly, thinking about his answers. This may be because his excellent English isn't as effortless as it seems, but it is more likely a sign of a methodical intelligence at work. He is happy to make light of his achievements, keen to demystify the process of movie-making but, at the same time, careful not to let too much of his guard down.

The Yin to his Yang (or should that be the other way round?) is Director of Photography and Australian émigré Christopher Doyle. My talk with him was quite a different experience. On one level he is a dream to interview because you hardly need to ask him any questions. On another level, his wit, knowledge and enthusiasm are quite exhausting. Sparkling with nervous energy, he couldn't just sit quietly and be interviewed so our conversation was recorded firstly in the back of a taxi, then as he elbowed his way through the markets and subways of downtown Hong Kong, his mobile phone stuck to one ear.

Together, Wong Kar-Wai and Christopher Doyle are the epitome of Strategy and Tactics, the former being a carefully considered long-term plan of action, the latter being the short-term tenacity and improvisational skill to bring those long-term plans to life. *Chungking Express* and *Fallen Angels* could not have been made without the perfect balance of both. Shot illegally on the streets of their neighbourhood in the Chungking district of Hong Kong, they set off, with a band of enthusiastic actors and no script, to re-energize the moribund Hong Kong film industry. Filming what they felt like, where they could, while the life of Britain's busiest principality spun and hustled blithely around them, they have brought a new spontaneity and vigour to the East.

Firstly, to ease you into the topsy-turvy world of Chungking Mansions, the calm and modulated words of director Wong Kar-Wai: I mentioned to him that I had seen *Chungking Express* and *Fallen Angels* on the same day, and felt that that was a particularly good way to see them!

"I think of *Chungking Express* as half and *Fallen Angels* as half." He explained, "Together they are one film. I had three short stories originally for *Chungking Express* but, because we filmed it in chronological order, I found that I was making it too long, so I skipped the third story. Then afterwards I thought well, maybe I can do another one. Not as a sequel but as a counterpart, so one character in *Chungking Express* can be projected into another character in *Fallen Angels*. Also, some of the smaller details, such as the uniform and the number 223."

And the all-night fast-food joint. That was the same one, wasn't it!?

"Yes, that is the *Chungking Express* take-away, where I got the title. It is part of Chungking Mansions, where the stories are set, so I had to reuse it in *Fallen Angels*. In fact, to me, the main character of these two films is Hong Kong itself, and the place never changes, but the stories change all the time. A different story happens in the same background. So we work like a closed-circuit camera, watching people going in and coming out, and the story just happens. They can be the same people or different people, it doesn't matter."

These films are very cinéma vérité: you seem to just shoot what's there, using available light.

"Yeah, that's because we have to work that way. It's the same situation as with the French New Wave in the 60s. We don't have much money. We have to finish the film very quickly, and normally we don't have street permits. The shops have their own lighting so, yes, we shoot what we find.

"We shot like this because I wanted a holiday after spending 2 years on *Ashes Of Time*. I needed a holiday but, instead of going someplace else, I decided to make a quick film. I didn't want a big cast or a big budget, I wanted to move around a lot and have fun. Everything was by instinct. I didn't have to consider and consider and consider a lot of elements like budget and scheduling. I wrote it and shot it in chronological order, usually writing in the daytime and shooting at night.

"Hong Kong is a very crowded place, so it would be quite impossible to make a film in that way in daytime. And I'm a night person anyway, that's when I'm at my best. The problem is that people have complained that I make Hong Kong look too quiet. Normally I have only one or two actors hanging around, it's a very quiet set. Except Hong Kong isn't like that."

You do show the contrast though: there's the crowded chaos of the opening scene of *Chungking Express* with everybody elbowing everybody else out of the way, compared to the shot out of the Killer's bedroom window in *Fallen Angels*, when you have acres of open concrete with nothing happening save the occasional elevated train rumbling past.

"This is my wish. I want to make Hong Kong seem bigger and quieter than it is. Really it's just like any other city. You'll see the MacDonalds, Circle K, 7-11 - this city has that, but every big city has that. So this story doesn't have to be in Hong Kong, it could as easily be in America or England.

"It is true that Hong Kong is maybe more cosmopolitan than most, that's why I chose Chungking Mansions as my location: there's over 200 guest houses in one single block, and something like 5,000 tourists from all over the world live in that space. It's very much like a small Hong Kong world, with a lot of people from many backgrounds living in a very limited space."

Why do you use the so-called 'smudge-motion' technique of shooting fewer frames per second so the action blurs?

"It's because I want to stop things down so that the things I want to concentrate on don't move while everything around them moves fast. Sometimes it's like trapping time. This is the magic of cinema, and the fun of being the director. You can change the time, you can play with time, but you can't in real life. You can be more real than real."

In a place that's so crowded, your films are full of lonely people. Is this your take on night in the city, or just people in the city?

"I think most people in a big city have a problem like this. Everyone is moving too fast, concentrating on their own business. And nowadays we have so many ways to communicate - we have phone, we have fax, pagers, e-mail. We have everything to make human contact more and more distant. It's like people would rather talk to a stranger over the phone in another city, than to meet that person personally."

So that is why Faye in *Chungking Express* engages in time-share relationship, only visiting her lover's house when he's out!?

"People are becoming more and more insecure, they don't want to get hurt. They want to protect themselves so they keep themselves to themselves. To avoid getting too lonely you have to know how to entertain yourself, even without a partner. My characters think they're communicating with each other, but they're not, so finally they decide that the most direct way to touch people or get hold of people is to share their houses."

It's a very pressurised environment, with a lot of stress. But the 2 gun-toting characters, who relieve their stress by shooting people - which are the 2 characters we in the West would most readily identify as being from a Hong Kong film - are as good as irrelevant to the main thrust of the plot.

"That's because I'm playing with the genre. The reason I originally wanted to have 3 short-stories in *Chungking Express* is because I wanted to include the cop, the gangster and the contract killer which are three of the main archetypes in Hong Kong film. So we have cops, but they're not supercops like Jackie Chan would play (so he doesn't have to worry about the competition). As for the killer in *Fallen Angels*, I wanted to introduce him in a way that makes you expect a John Woo film, with a big shoot out. But it was only interesting to me if I could follow it up with having him go home on the bus and meet an old school friend who tries to sell him insurance. What an anticlimax!

"Of course, it was important that the school-friend be played by the action director, who'd choreographed the shoot out and rigged all the special effects. You see, I'm trying to give you a surprise. It's like I'd given you a MacDonalds but when you unwrap it you realise it is really a Chinese dumpling! It's good to put your crew in your films because in years to come you can look at it and say, 'My God, you look so young! Where did it all go?' It's a punishment.

"This isn't just me being difficult though. It's a strategy to get the film seen. Normally the distributors here in South East Asia will ask, 'Do you have action in your film?' And I can say, 'Yes.' 'Do you have cops?' Of course I have a cop, but my cop is quite different. 'Do you have gangsters and gunfights?' Yes I do, but it's done differently.

"Sometimes the audience goes along with it, sometimes it fails. In *Fallen Angels* the audience is usually laughing when the killer gets on the bus, because they've been watching shoot-outs like that for so many years it has almost become a ceremony. When the killer meets his school friend, it tells them that he is real, a human being.

"Lately, of course, for the last 2 years or so, the 200 action films that the Hong Kong studios produce each year have been less popular than the big-budget Hollywood films, with their bigger special effects and bigger explosions but I think this is because films like the *Die Hard* series are more and more like Hong Kong films."

And many of your contemporaries - like Ringo Lam and John Woo - have moved to the States to make those bigger films. Are you planning to join them?

"No. You must remember that Ringo and John have always dreamed of working in Hollywood. I've known them since I worked in the script factory and they've always wanted to make at least one big Hollywood film. But that's not my dream.

"To be able to work I have to know the place, and know the people I am working with. My crew is like my family. Chris Doyle and I have worked together since my second film, so we know each other very well. Sometimes Chris says we're not like film-makers, we're like musicians at a jam session. I'm the band leader and everyone is jamming. I don't know enough musicians in the States. And can you imagine it, if they tried to re-make *Chungking Express* in America? They'd spend millions building Chungking Mansions again so they could light it properly, and then cast Tom Hanks as Tony Leung."

How do you respond to the parodies that are made of your films, like *Days Of Being Dumb*?

"We had to stop shooting *Ashes Of Time* for a few months so the cast could go off and film a parody of it, even before we'd finished. You have to be philosophical about it. I don't mind them, but I don't want to see them, that's all. I'm not against them, but I don't like them so I won't buy a ticket."

In the résumé they sent me, it mentions that you are perpetually wearing widescreen shades, in order to see the world through a cinema screen...

"Well that's only when I work. It's kind of my uniform. I'm not normally used to public speaking, so it's comforting to have dark glasses to hide behind but also, on set, it means that I can sleep and nobody notices. I just sit in my chair and people think I'm considering something, deep in thought. Just so long as I don't snore."

Well, I'll try to track down your director of photography now. I rang him before you but, since I was running behind schedule I think he must have gone to bed.

"No, I don't think so, the night is yet young for him!"

Christopher Doyle

Indeed, when I rang Chris Doyle, he wasn't sitting fretting by the phone, he'd gone out. However, he had left an answerphone message, in English: "Hello anyone calling, I have to go out for a moment but please try my mobile phone number .... byyyeee." This I dutifully did.

"Ah, you got my message then, good. I had to go out 'cos I'm late for a whole load of things but I'm in a cab, so we can talk."

I gather you're heading off to Argentina very soon ...

"Yes, I'm taking a cab to Argentina right now! No, okay, we're setting off in about three days."

And what techniques are you planning to use in this new f -

"Aaah, good question. I won't know until we get there. You know, when we shot *Days Of Being Wild*, I did 10 camera tests to find this nostalgic look we wanted. We didn't wanna use sepia, so I tried everything. First of all that sent the producer crazy because no one's ever done so many tests before in Hong Kong, and secondly Wong Kar-Wai would always say 'yeah, it's good, but this is still missing, and that is missing.' So, after 10 tests they wouldn't let me do any more, but we knew exactly what we didn't want. It wasn't until the first day of shooting that we found the right mix and got exactly what we did want and it was a great relief.

"It's the same thing this time. We can't use step printing, the so-called 'smudge-motion' technique, because that's been done to death now by everybody. Every film released here looks like a homage to Wong Kar-Wai. Even the music videos look like my assistant shot them ... it's horrible. So, for now, the look will rely on what the location gives us.

"I do like to hand-hold the camera, and he likes to just see what happens, so why work against it if it's working for you!? I dunno why, but it's extremely comfortable for me to hand-hold a camera. It gets things done quicker and more directly and gives you more time for an extra take without having to stop and relay the tracks and move the dolly - I just adapt my footwork. So that aspect, I don't see any need to change. But how that works within the whole context of how we use colour or processing or lighting, that will be determined by the space itself.

"As far as I'm concerned, that's what has become more and more evident the more we make films together. We trust each other more now, and we both trust that our choice of location will give us a direction on the look of the movie. It's what Buenos Aires gives us, not what we take to Buenos Aires. Unfortunately, Buenos Aires hasn't given me much so far. It's so bloody grey and European, and they still haven't worked out what happened after the tango. So I think we'll have to put a bit of energy in there to get anything out of the place.

"Have you ever been there?"

No, I ne -

"It's very weird, that's for sure. Everyone seems to have an identity crisis. They still think they're Italians or Spaniards or Nazis. Still, it doesn't matter, we'll all speak such beautiful Spanish by the time we've finished. That's why we're going really, for Spanish lessons, not to make a film! Hey, that's what we'll do. We'll structure the film like a Spanish language lesson. That's it, you've found the direction.

"In *Ashes Of Time*, we spent a year in the desert. I had three assistants carried back to civilisation in hospital chairs. It was extremely gruelling and yet, when we found the right space ... after something like eight months of shooting ... well that makes up something like 60% of what we see. It's amazing and very intuitive and inspires the horribly poetical metaphor that Wong Kar-Wai's films are really like sculpting, always taking away instead of adding.

"I'm always running around in circles all the time and he's so slow and analytical. And then you add in William Chang's design and editing, looking at it from an art director's point of view but also having a great complicity with me. I think it's a wonderful triad. A real triad. If you want me to sit down and watch the monitors I'd go crazy. I have to be up and running around with the camera.

"That was the problem when I first started shooting Chen Kaige's *Temptress Moon*. He's used to standing beside the monitor and being very analytical. I can't do that. I have to have the camera in my hand because then, when I'm exhausted enough, something interesting happens. And that's when Wong Kar-Wai, sitting there with his dark glasses on says, 'Is that all you can do, Chris?'

"For me it's very much a process based on the energy of the place. More and more the locations determine what we film. After all, I never know the story, so I can concentrate on other things. I think our 'greatest contribution' if you will, to local film-making is coherence of space, which is such a classic thing, a simple thing. But now everyone shoots around my neighbourhood - you know I live in the apartment where we shot *Chungking Express* - and everyone uses it because they think it's a coherent space. Which is true, but only once you've discovered it. They should go off and discover somewhere else.

"Look at *Fallen Angels* and all those confined spaces. No matter how much you theorise about things like 'oh, there's a distance between these people therefore we'll use a wide-angle lens to make them seem further apart than they really are,' - which is a great thing to write in a film journal and teach film students at the London Film School. But the reality is that we didn't have much space. We wanted to try something different. Wide-angle lenses looked okay, so we went with it. That's it! Then the film evolves day-by-day because you make stylistic choices about the acting style, the directorial style, the mise en scène etc., as you go along. At least between the three of us, the Wong Kar-Wai triad, that's very much how it works, and it's a very comfortable way of working."

And so -

"You know, you start from day one and it becomes a process. I'm terrified when western film-makers say 'we'd really like you to shoot our film but we only have 6 weeks, 2 weeks of prep ... oh, and a storyboard!' And I'm thinking: 'Shit, what am I gonna do? I don't even know you, how are we going to make a film together?'

"I get approximately a script a month now that I'm flavour-of-the-month, and they all expect another *Chungking Express*. But *Chungking Express* can only happen because of that collaboration, because of that space, because of that energy, because of that working style. Now, if you want me to imitate it, first of all I don't see the interest and secondly, why? Why do you want to do it? So I've been getting a lot of offers lately, and I hesitate because I'm not sure what they think I am. And secondly I'm not sure what they think I'm going to give them. And thirdly I don't know them, so I always say, 'well at least let's meet each other.'

"For me, for example, Chen Kaige or Stanley Kwan or any of the people I've worked with have been friends first before they became collaborators. Maybe I should test myself, but I'm a little hesitant because it's always been the people who have been the motivating force for me to take on a project, rather than a script. To be honest, I can't tell the difference between a good script and a bad script. It all looks horrible on paper, but hopefully it'll be a wonderful experience on film. For me the key has always been the experience and the process, and that means the people.

"I will be taking some western projects, even a Hollywood project next year. But that's also with people I've known for a long time. The script is totally secondary. That's the good ... or bad ... effect of working with Wong Kar-Wai. It's not planned. It's not an academic exercise. Which, of course, has its great dangers in terms of Hong Kong film-making. I assume we should move on, work out a more disciplined process, maybe. Or we could just keep the costs down and continue working like this, where it takes a year to finish a film but it's gonna be something interesting. I'm torn between the two! I'm getting old, so I'd prefer the shoots to be shorter, but my experience and personality are more of the 'let's just go for it' school."

I know there's an exhibition of your photographs being arranged in Rotterdam, and they're mostly taken behind-the-scenes while you're filming ...

"Let me try to explain. I'm kind of hyper, in case you hadn't noticed yet, and I have to have something to do otherwise I'm gonna jerk off five times a day. I have my wonderful team to work with, you know. I tell my lighting people what I want and they arrange it all, so I have a little time on my hands. I carry this little SLR camera in my pocket and I just wander around and if anything catches my eye I take pictures of it. It's become a wonderful obsession actually. So much so that last month I had a book released in Taiwan. This month I have one released here. I have two in Japan ... it's all becoming a little overwhelming. The problem is it's very easy to take the photographs but extremely difficult to organise them afterwards.

"I take them because, first of all, a lot of people don't know what goes on on a film set. Secondly, there's a lot of stuff that catches my eye, and I think I should train my eye as I go along. Thirdly, it just keeps me occupied while I'm waiting for other people to catch me up."

And -

"I've got this incredible accumulation of images now, which I've just got to get out of the house, because I'm using up an incredible amount of my energy just editing these photographs for exhibition."

I was wondering if they were just snaps of your friends from work.

"Oh very much so! They are just snaps, but they're useful because they're practice. It's like language. You practise, practise, practise and suddenly you say something that you didn't know you knew how to say. You realise that you can do something that you couldn't do before. I hope that the photography is the same. After all, it's not the machinery that's important, it's the atmosphere. I guess I've always self-trained, but that's because I think it's important to see where you're going, and how far you've come.

"Then, of course, it's a film-making situation, and a lot of people are involved that the public seem to be interested in, and you can see strange things happening that most people have never witnessed before. So it's an exciting experience to be able to share this kind of stuff.

"But yeah, they're snaps of the family. It just happens that my family is a film family. They just happen to be superstars, so, of course people are interested. Then maybe some of the images will be seen as human documents. I get trapped between deciding whether to release only the arty-farty stuff, or show people the superstars and the process. I'm always in two minds. Problem is, if I let someone else edit them, then I might find out that neither of them are intrinsically interesting.

"Actually, I do much more collage work than photography. It's sort of Post Withdrawal Syndrome Therapy. After 20 hours of filming, having to take care of 30 people who are directly answerable to me, and a 100 extras, and listening to Wong Kar-Wai moaning ,'Is that all you can do?' to just go home and cut up pieces of a magazine and put it with other pieces of another magazine to see what works, that's great therapy."

Some people go out and get drunk, you make collages!

"Oh I get drunk while I'm making collages. Or I get drunk first."

Tell me about Du Kefong.

"Du Kefong has no ID card, thank God, otherwise he'd have been in jail long ago. Du Kefong is a wonderful alter-ego, 'cos, first of all, his mother doesn't know what the hell he's doing. My mother's a raving Catholic. If she knew half of the shit Du Kefong gets up to ... I'm convinced she still thinks I'm a virgin, by the way. He makes a total ass of himself on stage, and wins all these awards, which is really strange, you know. But at least he doesn't take the awards home, because he usually loses it in the cab because he's so drunk.

"So Du Kefong is either a great burden, a great responsibility or a great liberation. It's great having him around. I'm very proud of him sometimes, and he gives me a great freedom that a lot of film-makers don't have, to just sit back and laugh.

"After several forays into the drug and esoteric religious cultures of the world, I ended up in Hong Kong, studying Chinese. My teacher was a wonderful, wonderful very beautiful poet, who knew I was in love with her and responded by giving me this beautiful name. 'Du' comes from Doyle, because it's traditional to make it sound like your English name, 'Ke' means 'like' and 'fong' means 'the wind.' So, supposedly this guy is like the wind, which is appropriate since I'm all over the place anyway. But also it comes from a classical expression which goes 'a gentleman is like the wind.' So it implies that this guy has an incredible amount of culture. [There is a pause here as Chris is gripped by hysterics for a few moments, before regaining - for want of a better term - composure]

"It's a very Chinese name. It's been something almost to live up to. Also it protects me from any prejudice that he might face if people really knew who the hell he is. He used to just go around making films, and people were used to the fact that some of the stuff he did was okay, and very Chinese, because they didn't know that he wasn't."

Was Christopher Doyle the well-digger, also the photographer?

"I dunno. Christopher Doyle is definitely the collage-maker. The well-digger ... yeah, he's probably the one character who is, because my form of camerawork is a great deal of physical effort, and a little bit of intellectual effort. That's the perfect balance for me. You want me sitting at home writing a book, no way. But you want me running around doing crazy things and thinking on my feet, yes, that's extremely appropriate. That's true to what I am and what I can do.

That's where the focal style and camerawork comes from. The fact that I like to dance has a much more direct relationship to the stylistic choices that I have made than any intellectualisation.

"I think I've done what I have done because I can, more than because we wanted to. The problem is that maybe we don't want to sometimes, but we can, what are we gonna do? Are we gonna negate the idea because we can, or because other people are imitating it? This is the question that has come up over the last couple of months as we prepare the next film.

"We've talked a lot about this, now that everyone is imitating our style. Then I did a short film with Wong Kar-Wai recently, just for Japanese release, and I've realised that it's okay. Firstly because we do it better than they do, because we know that it's not about the movement, it's about the pauses. I hope it's like music, I hope it's like poetry, the rhythm is there, the spaces between the notes are there. I hope that's what we're doing. I think we know more about the spaces between the notes than the people who just see our rhythms and try to imitate them. So I've become more reassured about that over the last few weeks, so what we do now is work on the other areas of the collaborations, which is the colour, the texture, the découpage, how the thing fits together, how we react to the actors, things like that.

"The real problem is that I don't have anyone pushing me. I don't feel that there's a new generation coming behind me, doing eye-opening work. I don't see people saying 'Fuck you, Chris. Fuck you Du Kefong, I can do better.' I just see people saying, that was a good idea, now I'll do it."

I gather the action movies that we know so well in the West are a dead art form in Hong Kong now.

"Well that's 'cos everyone's moving to Hollywood, isn't it? No, it's not a dead art form, it can't be. It's rejuvenated itself many, many, many times over the last 50 years, since the war. It's interesting that Shanghai used to be the centre, and now it's Hong Kong, and soon it'll be Shanghai again. I think it's basically just the same people moving back and forth across the border.

"What's popular locally is teenage gang stories. It's an evolution of the martial-arts genre, with young people who don't necessarily have much martial arts training going round doing a similar thing. In *Ashes Of Time* we tried very hard to evolve the genre, but I think that, until there's new blood, there won't be any surprises."

Chungking Express and *Fallen Angels* remind me of *A Bout De Souffle*, which led to the French New Wave. Maybe it's time for a Hong Kong New Wave?

"Hmm. I don't know if we were as reactionary as Godard. Maybe conceptually, but I don't think the local industry is anything like as strong as the French industry was at that time, not so entrenched in its own ways. A lot of our industry was already falling apart before we came on the scene. I think we were more intuitive than reactionary, which is a very Chinese way. I don't think Wong Kar-Wai is as aggressive as Godard. He's very discreet about the way he's doing things. When we work it is obvious that there's no holds barred, there's no question about that. While we were shooting our first film together, I thought that either it would be great or neither of us would make a film again. It really was intellectual guerrilla tactics. He is extremely driven and that's contagious. That's why his favourite saying to me is, 'Is that all you can do, Chris?'

"When you've been working 36 hours straight and you're exhausted because you've been running around with 30 kilograms of camera on your shoulder, and you've been hanging upside down suspended from a rope out of a window in order to get that shot, to have him say 'Is that all you can do?' kinda reminds you that film-making should be 100% attention to 100% of what's happening 100% of the time. And no excuses. Don't fuck off no matter how tired you are."

Heroic Bloodshed Filmography
Reviews by Paul Duncan.

As Tears Go By (1988)
Dir: Wong Kar-Wai. Cast: Andy Lau, Maggie Cheung, Jacky Cheung.

This is a retelling of Martin Scorsese's *Mean Streets* as if Scorsese was born and raised in Hong Kong rather than Little Italy.

Andy Lau takes on the Harvey Keitel role of the straight-as-an-arrow, hard-as-nails hoodlum who is constantly bailing out the soft-in-the-head Robert De Niro character, here played by Jacky Cheung. Delicate Maggie Cheung is the romantic interest, a shy cousin who shows Lau that life can be lived away from the Triads.

After Lau has saved Jacky several times and finally, sickened by the violence, retires to lick his wounds and live with Maggie, Jacky is embarrassed and takes on a suicide mission to show he is not afraid, that he can be a big man, that he deserves respect. Lau must make a decision, either to help his best friend or stay with the love of his life.

This is distinguished from other action movies by the realistic violence - hitting people hurts and has consequences - and the genuine emotion between the characters.

94m, Widescreen, Remastered Subtitles, Made In Hong Kong, 18 ☆☆☆☆☆

Days Of Being Wild (1991)

Dir: Wong Kar-Wai. Cast: Leslie Cheung, Maggie Cheung, Carina Lau, Andy Lau.

This is not a crime film. There are a couple of fight sequences but that's it.

This is not a love story - it's an unlove story. It's the story of a man who was abandoned by his mother, given to another woman for adoption, and who now revenges himself on all women by making them fall for him then rejecting them.

This is a beautifully touching film of unrequited love, of missed opportunities and of hate.

Languid people. Richly coloured rooms. Sticky damp heat. Unreservedly recommended.

94m, Widescreen, Subtitles, Made In Hong Kong, 12 ☆☆☆☆☆

Chungking Express (1994)

Dir: Wong Kar-Wai. Cast: Brigitte Lin, Takeshi Kaneshiro, Tony Leung Chiu Wai, Faye Wong, Valerie Chow.

Two stories are linked by a place: Chungking Mansions. The first story sees cop 223 fall in love with a blonde-wigged drug dealer. The second has a cop in love with an air hostess, who rejects him, and he fails to see that a girl at a fast-food store is in love with him - she occupies his apartment whilst he is not there.

These are thin stories no matter how you look at them. However, these stories are not about plot but about moments in time. How long do you wait for your love to be requited? What are the seconds, the minutes, the hours like? What fantasies enter your mind?

This film is shot with neon-bright colours. The predominant stylistic device is the so-called 'smudge-motion' - as the central character moves, he remains in focus whilst the rest of the picture becomes blurred.

Bewitching and emotional involving.

100m, Subtitles, ICA, 12 ☆☆☆☆☆

Fallen Angels (1995)

Dir: Wong Kar-Wai. Cast: Leon Lai, Michelle Reis, Takeshi Kaneshiro, Charlie Yeung, Karen Mok.

This is a companion piece to *Chungking Express*. There are two couples. The first are a hit man who likes to follow orders, and the female partner he has never met who tells him whom to kill. She is in love with him. The second pair are a man who wants to make people happy (so he takes over shops at night and forces people to try his products), and a woman wrapped up in her own world forever crying on the man's shoulder. He is in love with her.

So, this is another case of people not recognising that they are loved, and that contentment is beside them ready to be plucked. The tragedy is, of course, that this love is never consummated.

The photographic style of the movie relies almost solely on wide-angle lens. This is psychologically correct since the characters see themselves as the centre of attention and everybody else is pushed to their peripheral vision.

As ever, the silence between the bullets, between the sobs, is suffused with longing.

★★★★

Non Heroic Bloodshed Filmography

Ashes Of Time (1994)

Happy Together (1997)

Beijing Summer (2000)

Body Count

We have done our damnedest to watch and review as many of the available Heroic Bloodshed movies as possible. The following are listed in alphabetical order for easy reference. Reviews by John Ashbrook (JA), John Costello (JC), Paul Duncan (PD), Steve Holland (SH), Colin Odell & Michelle Le Blanc (C&M).

Chinese Untouchables (1994)

Dir: David Lai. Cast: Andy Lau, Cherie Chan, Damien Lau.

Hong Kong cinema's capacity to exploit any piece of cinema that has the potential to create a whole new film is unsurpassed. But if the final product is good, who cares? *Chinese Untouchables* is, as one might guess, a version of Brian de Palma's 1987 classic set in, wait for it, Shanghai with, don't tell me, opium dealing replacing good old prohibition. Andy Lau plays Cheung Ye-Pang, as straight an anti-drugs officer as it's possible to be. He has a pretty, understanding and pregnant wife, teams up with an ageing policeman, addict Cat, and a suicidal chopstick-wielding secret agent ready to expose the underground drugs trade run by the very pillars of society who have employed him.

The film-makers have splendidly recreated old Shanghai, but haven't balked on the action or violence. The hardware may be old-fashioned, but there's plenty of it, including the world famous "gun of a thousand bullets" and some very lethal sticks of dynamite. The action is fast-paced and the stunts exciting - the waterslide at the drugs factory looks like a potential theme park attraction and there is a sobering warning not to get caught in revolving doors. It looks gorgeous throughout - many scenes were shot in a muted sepia tone - and the fluid camerawork suitably complements the changing pace. But the main reason this film is so good is the sense of tragic inevitability. Another rule of HK cinema is that Andy Lau should never be allowed to have an easy time - he is constantly tortured and abused for our entertainment and this is no exception. But we love him for it, the masochistic old devil!

100min, Widescreen, Subtitles, Eastern Heroes, 18 ★★★★ C&M

The Club (1981), Rock N Roll Cop (1994)

The Club Dir: Kirk Wong. Cast: Chan Wai Man, Tsui Siu Keung, Kent Cheng, Cheung Kuen, Ko Fei, Wilson Tong, Kwan Young Moon.

Rock N Roll Cop Dir: Kirk Wong. Cast: Anthony Wong Chow-Sun, Yu Rong-Guang, Wu Xing-Guo (Ng Hing-Kwok), Carrie Ng Ka-Lai, Chan Ming-Chun, Yau Kin-Kwok.

Kirk Wong has one of those curious places amongst British fans - a hero before his movies actually appeared on these shores. Jackie Chan fans knew that *Crime Story* was his serious movie, but how many people had actually seen it until its release by 20:20 Vision in 1995? Wong's notoriety had spread a year earlier and had already gathered plenty of momentum by the time Channel 4 showed *Rock N Roll Cop* and Eastern Heroes released *The Club*. Those three movies remain the most accessible to fans and make an interesting study. Of the three, *The Club* may be the least typical but as Wong's first movie it laid down a code which Wong has travelled and embellished ever since. Centred around and set in a Hong Kong nightclub run by a small gang Uncle, the club itself becomes the target for a property developer. But when the boss of the club tries to lever more money and a position on the board from triad boss Wah Shun using blackmail, he ends up dead. Caught in the middle of a bloody battle is brother Sai, played by one-time real-life gangster Chan Wai Man, whose physicality and triad tattoos make him an imposing figure amongst even the seasoned stunt men he dispatches. The plot which drives the movie is ever present, as are the every day problems Sai faces - which he inevitably deals with violently. This was filmed long before John Woo reinvented the triads in *A Better Tomorrow*, and shows none of the sentimentality of later Hong Kong action movies. Revenge is a simple motive, escalating in Sai as more of his friends and colleagues are killed until he erupts in barbaric mayhem. Based partly on a true story, as was *Crime Story*, Wong succeeds in making a fictionalised fly-on-the-wall documentary, intruding into every nook and cranny of the nightclub life, particularly that of Hong Kong's famed hostesses.

Rock N Roll Cop (Literal Chinese Name: Provincial Harbor Number One Offender All Points Bulletin) stars Anthony (*Bunman*) Wong as Inspector Hong, an undercover cop who travels to mainland China to round up a gang of crooks who are already known to the police of the people's Republic as the Red Scarf Gang. The cat and mouse game of tracking down gang boss Shen pitches Hong against his counterpart, Captain Wang: Hong boasts about the technology available to Hong Kong police, and flaunts his lone-wolf, anything goes attitude. Wang, methodical and resourceful, eventually has to send Hong back to Hong Kong; Hong spots a number of cops following Shen's girlfriend across the border and returns to work with Wang in finding the gang. When Shen is finally captured and accompanies Hong, the two handcuffed together, across the border, only to be freed by two colleagues. Only in these latter moments of the movie does Hong realise that Wang has been tied down by the same bureaucracy that he himself finds so frustrating in Hong Kong. Shen's girlfriend, it is discovered, is also Wang's ex-girlfriend, whom Shen kills. Shen has also been responsible for the death of Wang's mentor, Master Leung (in the film's extremely violent opening scenes). Wang crosses the line - the border - to save Hong and the two find hope that, come 1997, they will be able to work together when the borders are finally dropped. This anti-bureaucracy attitude seems typical of Kirk Wong's films. It's the same in *Crime Story*, although muted since it is a vehicle for Jackie Chan; Wong seems to distrust authority, believing it corrupt and immoral. Those cops who hit the streets for low pay but with pride in their badge are the heroes, and if they need to use violence to achieve results, so be it. Once unleashed, they become relentless, and whether you hold with that as moral or not, it makes for exciting viewing in a movie.

The Club, 81m, Remastered Subtitles, Eastern Heroes, 18 ★★★★ SH

Code Of Honour (1989)
Dir: Benny Chan. Cast: Dick Wei, Chow Yun Fat, Danny Lee, Ko Chun Hsiung.

Despite having retired ten years ago, top triad boss Ho (Ko) still keeps his hand in by preventing three main rival factions from doing too much damage to each other. His son Ray (Chow) wants him to sever his criminal ties and join his family in Australia, something Ho wants to do but as loyalty comes first, feels obliged to run down his operations before leaving. Inspector Mak (Wei) wants Ho in the slammer, citing the now charitable 70 year old as responsible for the death of his father. Inevitably, his unorthodox methods do not win him the praise of his superiors. With his brother crippled trying to get undercover information, Mak persuades witnesses to testify against Ho but, wouldn't you know, they get bumped off. Undeterred he uses illegal immigrant Sally to help him get the venerable gangster behind bars. But, with Ho's bags already packed for a move Down Under, someone is going to end up dissatisfied.

Benny Chan's film is a dark (literally - half the time you can't see what's going on) lament for an ageing gangster and a bitter policeman living in the shadow of his father. Breaking ties sometimes means breaking loyalties. Ho's character is genuinely seeking redemption, but for Mak this is not enough. Punctuating these themes are scenes of graphic violence, enhanced by the grainy cinematography, which make a sobering film that is brutal but never sensationalist. Sadly, whatever the quality of the original version, the video suffers the indignities of poor transfer, bad dubbing and two minutes of censorship from the BBFC. Claiming it 'stars' Chow Yun Fat and Danny Lee is a bit rich too...

86m, MIA, 18 NN C&M

The Corruptor (1999)

Dir: James Foley. Cast: Chow Yun Fat (Lt Nick Chen), Mark Wahlberg (Danny Wallace), Brian Cox (Sean Wallace).

It is my considered opinion, that Heroic Bloodshed partly arose in Hong Kong from a desire to redress the imbalance created by the Hollywood action movie *Year Of The Dragon* (1985); by borrowing its violence and the police-procedural structure, but adding the 'revolutionary' concept that the Chinaman could also be the hero!

Now that the genre has emigrated and become Hollywood Bloodshed, it could be payback time! By rights, we should be entering an all-new, big-budget, epic phase in HB's development. Although *The Corruptor* is far from realising this dream, it's a start.

Mark Wahlberg plays the token white guy, foisted onto a Chinatown unit run by Chow, and quickly introduced to the way things work there. "You don't change Chinatown," He is told, ominously, "It changes you!" He is our Willard, leading us down the river into the heart of Chinatown's darkness. It's not exactly a revolutionary framework, we've seen it any number of times before. But, in this densely-plotted spinning of the tale, there are enough twists and turns to keep even the most jaded viewer's eyes peeled.

Foley, who excelled as the director of *At Close Range* (1985) and *Glengarry Glen Ross* (1992), has, probably wisely, opted for copying Ringo Lam's trade-mark hand-held, neon-lit style, with occasional swoops and crash-edits to keep the MTVideots from getting too twitchy.

For those who like a little sociology in their HB, this film tasks you to decide whether the corrupter of the title is the law enforcement system, or Chinatown itself. For those who prefer blood and snot, there's some very squelchy shoot-outs and one extraordinarily well-crafted car chase. So, fun for all the family.

110m, New Line, 18 ★★★ JA

Crime Story (1993)

Dir: Kirk Wong. Cast: Jackie Chan, Kent Cheng, Christine Ng, Law Hang Kang.

I love this film. A Chinese businessman is kidnapped, and held for ransom. Jackie Chan, in a serious role, is the cop assigned to track down the kidnappers, unaware that his partner is one of them. At every turn Jackie is outfoxed. Based on a true story, this still delivers lots of realistic gunfights on the streets, car stunts on the roads and chases over rooftops. At one point, I was sure that Michael Mann had seen this film and used scenes in *Heat*. All-in-all, it is a pity that Kirk Wong is not better known, and it is a great shame that many of his other Hong Kong films have not managed to get a Western release.

105m, MIA, 18 ★★★★ PD

Guns Of Dragon (1995)

Dir: Tony Leung. Cast: Ray Lui, Steven Darrow, Mark Cheung.

Officer Tony Lam (Ray Lui) arrives in New York, from Hong Kong, nurturing his letter of resignation from the force. Noticing his occupation, the Customs Official asks if he has his gun. "No, I hear anyone can get a gun in the United States." "That's right," admits the official, ruefully, "That's why you should have yours."

The plot is fairly representative - Tony Lam, legendary triad-buster back home, arrives in the States to make peace with his émigré wife. "You're a good cop," she informs him at one point, "But you'll never be a good husband or father." To this, he tells her of his resignation...but who should turn the corner and spot him, The Gangster Formerly Known As Prince, Tony's long-time nemesis. It would seem that the triads, in common with their prey, are relocating to America.

It is fascinating to watch the trademark Hong Kong action sequences played out in the New York streets. It makes you realise that, once the exodus is complete and Hong Kong's action men are firmly established in the US, actors like Bruce Willis are gonna have to spend a lot of time and trouble brushing up their martial arts skills if they are to keep up with their new directors' demands.

So, in keeping with the new tradition (if you can have such a thing) of Hong Kong movies, *Guns Of Dragon* has a distinctly international flavour, with settings in New York and Puerto Rico. Indeed, not one foot of film was shot in Hong Kong itself. It employs bilingual dialogue more effectively than any other Hong Kong film I have seen (including Jackie Chan's made-f or-America *Rumble In The Bronx*) and, as such, serves as a tremendous calling card for director Leung, previously best known as an actor who has obviously learned a thing or two from The Greats. I look forward to his next chance to demonstrate that knowledge.

90m, MIA, 18 ★★★ JA

Hard Boiled 2:The Last Blood (1991)

Dir: Wong Jing. Cast: Andy Lau, Alan Tam, Eric Tsang, Leung Kar Yan.

If *Bullet In The Head* is John Woo's tribute to American movies, then *The Last Blood* is Wong Jing's tribute to John Woo movies. One that I'm sure he can live without.

Hong Kong's er, relaxed attitude to copyright is responsible for numerous fakes of all kinds: clothes, perfumes, jewelry etc. *Hard Boiled 2* has no connection to John Woo's *Hard Boiled*, just as the same director's *Return To A Better Tomorrow* has nothing to do with the original trilogy. These films are nothing more than an attempt to cash in on John Woo's reputation, but these fakes are, like most, inferior copies of the real thing.

This video release on the Eastern Heroes label promises that *The Last Blood* has '...all the trademarks and high body count of a John Woo movie.' Unfortunately, the trademarks are ripped-off action replays and the body count is reached via far less style and panache.

The film is technically proficient, but the premise is the height of absurdity: the plot, such as it is, concerns the attempts of a Japanese suicide squad to assassinate religious leader Daka Lama (!) as he arrives in Singapore for the Nation Day celebrations. Daka Lama is wounded in the attempt, as is small-time hood Andy Lau's girlfriend. She and the Lama are somehow spiritually connected and share the same, highly unusual, blood group. The race is on for Lau and cool cop Alan Lam to find a suitable donor for transfusion as the terrorists target all possible donors to stop them. Will their uneasy alliance save the day, or will the fanatical Saporo emerge triumphant?

The response from this reviewer was: who cares? Seen it all before, much better done.

The narrative is confused and the dialogue risible, not served well by the subtitles which are often hilarious: a mysterious organisation called Interpo is mentioned more than once, and the following exchange is not untypical:

"Who is upstairs?"

"No."

"Are there another woman?"

If this sounds bad, it is only because I have failed to convey its true awfulness. Do yourself a favour. Watch *Hard Boiled* (or any John Woo movie) instead.

90m, Widescreen, Subtitles, Eastern Heroes, 18 ☆ JC

Man Wanted (1994)

Dir: Cheung Bing, Chen Mok Sing. Cast: Simon Yam, Yu Rong Kwong, Christy Chung.

This has the Category III sign all over the cover. I have no idea why - there is no nudity, and the violence is not particularly goresome. Perhaps it's Cat III because it took me three attempts before I could sit through it all.

Simon Yam plays an up and coming triad member, close confidante of his boss, ruthless Yu Rong Kwong. When they are trapped by the police, it turns out Yam is an undercover cop, and he finds his loyalties divided between friendship and duty. When Kwong dies, Yam feels both responsible to Kwong's girlfriend and is guilty about being in love with her. Eventually, Kwong resurfaces and wreaks havoc - cue violent gunfest.

Hong Kong action movies often have one or two illogical gaps in their stories. I have no objection to these gaps as long as I understand the motivation of the characters - I can live with emotion winning over logic. I didn't feel as though I knew the characters in *Man Wanted*. They tried so hard, emoting all over the place, leaving long pauses for a meaningful song to be inserted - Michael Mann and *Miami Vice* have a lot to answer for.

There is one interesting sequence about two-thirds through where Simon Yam is injected with drugs, has a gun taped to his hand and runs through the streets, hallucinating, seeing cops as robbers, shooting them - but I've seen the rest of it elsewhere, better done.

90m, Widescreen, Subtitles, Eastern Heroes, 18 ★★ PD

A Moment Of Romance (1990)

Dir: Benny Chan. Cast: Andy Lau, Ng Sin Liang, Chan Ah Lun.

Now, tell me if this seems familiar. Andy Lau takes on the Harvey Keitel role of the straight-as-an-arrow, hard-as-nails hoodlum who is constantly bailing out the soft-in-the-head Robert De Niro character, here played by Chan Ah Lun. Delicate Ng Sin Liang is the romantic interest, a shy teenager, kidnapped by Lau during a robbery, who shows Lau that life can be lived away from the triads.

Okay, it's not the same as Wong Kar-Wai's *As Tears Go By*, or even Martin Scorsese's *Mean Streets*, but there are more similarities than differences. Andy Lau, once again, plays the ill-fated rebel trapped in a world he never made. You know that he will die in the end, only how he dies is in doubt.

On the plus side are some visually stunning sequences, good production values, editing, and acting.

88m, Widescreen, Subtitles, Made In Hong Kong, 18 ★★★ PD

A Moment Of Romance II (1993)

Dir: Benny Chan. Cast: Aaron Kwok, Wu Chien Lien, Kwok Tsun On, Anthony Wong.

Celia is working in Hong Kong illegally to raise $50,000 to free her brother who has been incarcerated for writing anti-corruption literature. Her career as a prostitute is curtailed by the brutal murder of the gangland boss she is meant to be entertaining, which forces her on the run from new leader Paul - the real murderer. Fortunately her path crosses with that of Frank, a bike racer who is estranged from his father because he feels responsible for the death of his mother. Also on Celia's tail is ice cream and mung bean lolly obsessed ageing policeman Billy. Further confounding problems is Jack, whose financial problems lead him to betray Frank in a race for the money that Celia so desperately needs. With racing grudges to contend with, Jack's redemption to consider, and the mob to be kept at bay, will true love last for Celia and Frank?

A Moment Of Romance II has only a titular connection with the first film. Aaron Kwok, teenage hearthrob that he is, wide-eyes his way admirably through the proceedings, while Wu Chien Lien's Celia exudes quiet desperation. They even find time for a number of cantopop ballads in between the nicely paced but relatively spartan plotting. Benny Chan's direction doesn't intrude and, while the body count is surprisingly low, there are some scenes of quite shocking violence and nicely understated romance - for just a moment of course. Tragic but likeable, pack some kleenex and watch out for those motorbikes.

88min, Cat II, ★★★ C&M

People's Hero (1987)

Dir: Derek Yee. Cast: Ti Lung, Tony Leung (Kar Fai), Tony Leung (Chui Wei), Chiu Pui.

This is not a wham-bam-thank-you-ma'm kinda movie. This has got real acting in it, with Ti Lung as Al Pacino in a variation of Sidney Lumet's *Dog Day Afternoon* (1975).

The plot is simple. Two punks go into a bank to rob it, change their minds then, when their rented gun is spotted, end up shooting the guard and have to go through with the robbery. They botch it badly

- get trapped inside with hostages, surrounded by armed police. Then, Ti Lung - a wanted man, a cop-killer, caught inside the bank just before catching his boat to freedom - pulls his gun on the would-be bank robbers and takes over.

Ti Lung, best known to heroic bloodshed fans for his *A Better Tomorrow* films, is masterful. Remember how Al Pacino, in *Carlito's Way*, controlled the screen, mesmerised us? Ti Lung is just as powerful here. He's having a bad day, no doubt about it.

Derek Yee's taut direction deserves praise. I'd certainly like to see more of his work, especially the award-winning *C'Est La Vie Mon Chéri* (1993).

(By the way, please notice that there are two Tony Leungs - one was in the John Woo films *Bullet In The Head* and *Hard Boiled*, the other was in *The Lover*. Please don't get them confused like everyone else does.)

Gripping from beginning to end, you won't notice the time slip away, or the fact that it's set in one room. One to savour.

90m, Widescreen, Subtitles, Eastern Heroes, 18 ★★★★ PD

Portland Street Blues (1998)

Dir: Raymond Yip Wai Man. Cast: Sandra Ng, Kirsty Yeung, Wan Chi Shing, Alex Fok, Ng Man Tat.

Thirteen (named after her father's lucky Mah Jong streak at her birth) and Yun use their close friendship to trick (literally) gullible males out of their money. They get in too deep with the appropriately named SOB, a bad triad who casually has Thirteen beaten and her father killed for their youthful treachery. Thirteen's poor attempts at revenge are dissipated by mask-wearing heroin addict Kei, whose corrupt police ex-lover is a reprehensible animal no better than SOB. After fleeing to China with Coke, a kickboxer for whom she has a schoolgirl crush, Thirteen eventually returns to Hong Kong and wins the respect of a triad group to become kingpin of Portland Street. Inevitably betrayals abound, but perhaps love and friendship can defeat the odds.

This is a spin-off to the *Young And Dangerous* series. Comparisons to Wong Kar-Wai, particularly *As Tears Go By*, are inevitable but this should not denigrate what is a powerful, well-scripted and well-acted drama. Scenes of extensive and shocking brutality punctuate long sequences of character development and introspection, resulting in a believable film that never shies but is not exploitative. Thirteen's lesbianism is never sensationalised or derided - indeed the film shows remarkable restraint in its honest depiction of all concerned. With unobtrusive direction and wide sound separation, this is a film to relish, occasionally shocking but always compelling.

114mins, Cat III, Widescreen, ★★★★ C&M

Return To A Better Tomorrow (1994)

Dir: Wong Jing. Cast: Michael Wong, Jeff Lau, James Wong, Chingamy Yau, Dior Cheng.

One-man film-factory Wong Jing's film has, as expected, no connection with the John Woo/Tsui Hark trilogy save for the fact that the title is just as ironic. Chun is a good triad, he does not do drugs, but he's not good enough to curtail the assassination of Black Ox at his cinema - thereby invoking the wrath of Ox's gang. Closer to home, someone has been implicating him in cocaine smuggling. Is it long-suffering girlfriend Chili who wants to go to Canada? Is it Lobster, comic book lover and gangster? His pretty daughter Little Lobster? His 'orrible wife or her grotty lover Tung the Scorched Bottom? Or Chiu? Is it mild mannered karaoke drunk Wei? Could be... Much swapping of bullets and swiping of machetes later, Chun has to hop across to China to escape, but it's a trap! Chui has an unfortunate encounter with an amputating hairdresser and gets to scream at the atrocious Geisha giggle of the highly unhinged Holland Boy. Chun returns two years later to confront his enemies and find his friends. Did we mention the missing digit, the heroin addiction, terminal disease, wedding plans or the reel-to-reel tape in the pizza? Thought not...

Never one to balk on the carnage, this is a typically bloody affair but never dull, with enough twists to have you shouting "Don't go in the...doh!" at the screen. Yes it's derivative and it overuses the Wong Kar-Wai blur-mo, but the showy technique, glossy colours and engaging characters make for cracking entertainment. Top marks for the excellent video transfer too.

99mins, Widescreen, Subtitled, MIA, 18 ★★★ C&M

Rich And Famous (1986), Tragic Hero (1987)

Dir: Taylor Wong. Cast: Chow Yun Fat, Andy Lau, Alex Man.

In his book *Hong Kong Action Cinema*, Bey Logan refers to these two films as offering 'all the bloodshed of *A Better Tomorrow* but less of the heroism' and, between them, they constitute an 'underrated gangster classic.' Like the first two *A Better Tomorrow* films, the rise and fall of a gangster empire, headed by Chow Yu.

Rich And Famous introduces us to Yung, his adopted brother, and their adopted sister Chui, as they and their father flee China to Hong Kong in the mass exodus of the early 50s. Fast forward to the 70s and Yung has turned into the black sheep of the family, running up gambling debts at the casino owned by the local Don, Mr Chai - played by a curiously paternal Chow Yun Fat. Chai takes the stray waifs under his wing and, eventually, decides to name them as his heirs, which promptly causes friction between the two brothers.

Tragic Hero begins with Yung, having taken to plastering his hair back with gel and grinning maniacally at every possible opportunity, running Chai's empire whilst Kwok, sick of fighting, has gone off to run a pub somewhere. But Yung, never one to know when he's won, continues to wage war against Chai, his benefactor.

Inevitably, the whole family gets drawn back together for a climatic showdown which owes not a little to Brian De Palma's *Scarface*. The films also draw inspiration from Sergio Leone's *Once Upon A Time In America* as well as Francis Ford Coppola's *The Godfather*, with a smear of Shakespeare's *King Lear* for good measure.

Character and plot developments are at a premium here, taking precedence over the big spectacular stunt sequences used by those who came later. However, possibly because these films are so methodically paced, the action/violence sequences are all the more effective when they do strike, particularly in *Tragic Hero*.

The films are most significant, however, for setting up themes which would sustain the Hong Kong action movie throughout the next decade: family loyalty and, by extension, betrayal; honour and sacrifice. *Rich And Famous* and *Tragic Hero* offer an opportunity to see Heroic Bloodshed in the days before it was even a genre, let alone a cliché.

Rich And Famous, 99m, Widescreen, Remastered Subtitles, Made In Hong Kong ★★★

Tragic Hero, 88m, Widescreen, Remastered Subtitles, Made In Hong Kong ★★★★ JA

Run And Kill (1993)

Dir: Billy Tang. Cast: Kent Cheng Tut Si, Simon Yam, Danny Lee, Esther Kwan.

Our hero, Fatty, catches his wife doing vertical exercises with some young upstart. Dejected, he seeks solace in a bar and becomes involved with a gang of unsavouries. His drunken mumblings are

...sunderstood, and the next day our porky pal arrives home to find wifey and boogie boy together, and the triad nutzoids about to fulfill the contract. The amorous duo are killed despite his protestations. Naturally the gang are miffed at his interference and want their dough. But our bumbling hero can't/won't cough up, so he leaves town. Staying at his secret pad are a band of fruitcakes led by prime headcase Simon Yam. Fatty persuades Simon's demented brother to beat up the first (marginally less) psycho gang. Five billion chaotic twists and sub-plots later results in everyone being pissed at Fatty, particularly Simon. The film then moves from yuppie nightmare into a whole new ballfield of unpleasantness. Simon gets down to some very nasty revenge that is so deranged they haven't found words for it yet. Needless to say, the psychological effect on Fatty, forced to watch these events in gruesome detail while simultaneously contending with Simon's outrageously poor puns, is immense. The stage is set for a *Terminator*-style showdown of catastrophic proportions.

This is a sick little bunny of a film - initially fairly conventional, it quickly spirals into gore-drenched insanity. What makes it good, apart from the diligent enthusiasm of all involved, is that it is so funny. Not in a belly laugh way but, as events escalate, the absurdity reaches such hysterical levels that the whole thing seems like Scorsese's *After Hours*, only with charred corpses and unimaginable violence. A delirious cocktail of a film - far better than its budget or reputation would lead you to expect. Don't watch on a full stomach or show this to elderly relatives though...

91min, Cat III, ★★★★ C&M

Shanghai Triad (1995)

Dir: Zhang Yimou. Cast: Gong Li, Li Baotian, Li Xuejian, Shun Chun, Wang Xiao Xiao.

30s Shanghai: bathed in sepia, smuggled dust settles on red floorboards.

Nightclub: white lights, skin gleaming, petal throat, Bijou's song like beads of honey.

Backroom: black, Boss, still, his mumbles roar, his shaded eyes probe.

Mansion: yellow, awkward boy tiptoes through the house of men.

Island: green, the wind blows but nobody listens.

Story: boredom, bed, betrayal, blood.

In a man's world, sex is bought by the power of violence.

112m, Widescreen, Subtitles, Electric, 15 ★★★★ PD

The Tigers

Dir: Eric Tsang. Cast: Andy Lau, Wong Yat Wah, Tony Leung, Leung Kar Yan, Tong Chen Yip.

This is not interesting. I tried my hardest to watch it all, but I ended up fast-forwarding through it to see if there was anything good I could say about it. There wasn't.

The story concerns five cops who, after a raid, take the money and are blackmailed by a gangster. They don't play ball, so the gangster shops them to internal affairs.

The characters are non-existent, unsympathetic - I did not know why they were doing things. The comedy wasn't funny. Worst of all, the fight scenes weren't very good. The blurb on the back says that the climatic fight will 'blow you away.' If you're expecting John Woo, I think this scene is more likely to 'piss you off.'

110m, Widescreen, Subtitles, Eastern Heroes, 18 ★ PD

To Live And Die In Tsimshatsui (1994)

Dir: Andrew Lau (aka Wai Keung Lau) & Wong Jing. Cast: Jacky Cheung, Roy Cheung, Tony Leung, Chien-Lien Wu.

This film is an interesting mix of 80s Hollywood slick (as exemplified by *Miami Vice* and, of course, *To Live And Die In LA*), and 90s docudrama. The evil police inspector Suen wears baggy white suits à la Sonny Crockett, whilst most of the set-pieces are accompanied by driving synth music, à la Harold Faltermeyer (remember him?) Yet, the images themselves are of washed-out neon landscapes, shot in available light by hand-held cameras; that very 90s signature of Chris Doyle and Ringo Lam.

Ah Lik (Jacky Cheung) is a detective, deep undercover in the heart of a triad family. Universally trusted and liked by all his gangster 'brothers,' whilst simultaneously threatened and abused by his police superiors, he begins to wonder where his loyalties really lie, and who, therefore, he really is.

We first meet him, gazing into the bathroom mirror, asking himself this. It is a pose he will assume repeatedly throughout the film, as the difference between good and evil becomes increasingly indistinct.

Quite early in the film's narrative, he watches flies disintegrating as they collide with a fluorescent blue fly trap. He wonders if he'll make a bright flash when he is drawn into the light.

Well, with the extreme violence flaring within the different factions of the gang, and the callous brutality of the police, you know it can't end well. Progressively, the tragedies that pile up around him, push Lik too far, and he finds himself severing the ties that hold his life together. He is determined to go out in a real blaze of glory.

Although more thoughtful than the pure blood-and-guts quickies of recent Heroic Bloodshed, this tale doesn't quite match up to the A-list of the genre, being a little too obvious and a lot too derivative. Nevertheless, a superb programme filler.

105m, ★★★ JA

Young And Dangerous (1995)

Dir: Andrew Lau. Cast: Dior Cheng (Ekin Cheng), Jordon Chan, Gigi Lia, Simon Yam.

Life in the triads begins at a young age as Nam and his school-friends are intimidated by Coke bottle wielding Kwan and they pledge their allegiance to Bee. Ten years later they are all part of the Hung Hing society, bumping off Ba-Bai with the aid of a fashionable hairdryer whilst still avoiding the loathsome Kwan. Nam starts dating the stammering Smartie who had previously tried to steal his car. After a set up at Macau gambling joint muscled in on by Crazy Bill's gang, Nam is drugged and filmed having sex with Chicken's girlfriend - Chicken at the time enjoying the company of three lovelies in a hotel room. Chicken lies low in Taiwan for a while and Nam, disgraced, faces the wrong end of a bundle of incense and sets up a café. Ten months later Nam returns to pay his respects to Bee and his family, who were brutally murdered by Kwan, and maybe he can reunite his triad buddies to seek their own special brand of justice.

Kau Man's *Teddy Boy* comics provide more than just the inspiration for Andrew Lau's surprise hit - they are woven intrinsically into the fabric of the film, serving as punctuation to the onscreen events as shots fade to cartoon. This also serves to emphasise that this is definitely not real life. It comes as some surprise that all this proves to be as far from a comic book adaptation as you are likely to see. Instead of the exaggerated excesses of the gangster film with its high body count and extreme emotions, *Young And Dangerous* offers us a relatively quiet drama with short bursts of violence, making for a far more believable and engaging tale. The combination of fashionable clothing, an easy-to-watch cast and nice haircuts proved to be box office gold. Four sequels, a prequel and a dozen spin-offs resulted.

98mins, Widescreen, Subtitled, MIA, 18, ★★★★ C&M

Young And Dangerous II(1996)

Dir: Andrew Lau. Cast: Dior Cheng (Ekin Cheng), Jordon Chan, Anthony Wong, Gigi Lia, Simon Yam, Chingamy Yau.

The Hung Hing boys are back in town. Nam is being pushed to become leader of Causeway Bay but doesn't count on nose-picking, medallion wearing wildman Fei who is also vying for the position. Events seem to be linked to Chicken's spell in Taiwan the previous year - his cousin Darkie introduced him to Mr Liu, an impotent San Luen triad leader. Chicken falls in love with Liu's girlfriend Yao, a treacherous manipulator who wishes to own a Macau casino. As the opening ceremony approaches, Nam is running out of luck - Smartie is in a coma, Yi has (under duress) betrayed him and new boy Banana Skin's wardrobe needs serious attention. But at least the crazy priest is still around to supply spiritual guidance…

The first film proved such a hit when it was released in January 1996 that two sequels were made and hit the cinemas before the summer of the same year! All three became top ten smashes. Director Lau also shoots his films - he started off as a cinematographer working for such talents as Wong Kar-Wai, Ringo Lam and Tsui Hark. The results are assured and only sporadically flashy (some great fast tracks!), Lau preferring to let the characters develop in soap opera style. In some respects this is more like *The Sopranos* but without the ugly cast or psychiatrist, while structurally it resembles *The Godfather Part II* but handles the temporal changes without resort to cliché. Compelling for its own sake this is not *A Better Tomorrow* for the 90s, it's a whole different game and far better for it.

96mins, Widescreen, Subtitled, MIA, 18, ★★★★ C&M

Young And Dangerous III(1996)

Dir: Andrew Lau. Cast: Dior Cheng (Ekin Cheng), Jordon Chan, Anthony Wong, Gigi Lia, Simon Yam.

Tung Sing triad boss Camel Lok and his intensely cocky sidekick Crow decide it's time for a more hands-on, or should that be hands off (ouch!), approach to running business. Fresh from Holland, they shamelessly invade Causeway Bay. Meanwhile, Smartie recovers from her coma but has amnesia, Chicken rejoins Hung Hing from the bottom and has to look after Shuk-Fan, the priest's bonkers daughter (advice: Don't buy your condoms in the same shop that your girlfriend's father frequents), and Chiang is in serious Dutch negotiations that could prove detrimental to the health of all and sundry. Crow and Tiger set up both Chicken and Nam, even some schoolkids manage to intimidate our cuddly buddies, and Banana Skin has not improved his wardrobe. Grim prospects all round…

Chicken gets the third different haircut on the trot but apart from that it's business as usual for our (relatively) mild-mannered triad friends. All fades to the comic have now vanished and there is a real sense that the series has settled in. This makes the unexpected deaths of two pivotal characters (we won't say which but don't read the cast list for part 4!) all the more jolting. Lau refers constantly to the film-making process (freeze frames, re-enactments of part one for Smartie's benefit, porno films) and occasionally questions Hong Kong's situation as 1997 approaches. Yes, the action is 'Western' pedestrian, when there is any at all, but that's to miss the point. If you're not addicted to the series by now check your pulse, you may be in for a shock…

98mins, Widescreen, Subtitled, Cat II, ★★★★ C&M

Resource Materials

Books & Magazines

Eastern Heroes Magazine

Long-established magazine about all things Hong Kongian contains interviews, features, reviews of films it'll probably take years to get on video, and news of upcoming films/events. Basically, it's essential to buy this magazine if you want to know what's what. There is a limited edition of the best of the first 19 issues - it includes Heroic Bloodshed interviews (Chow Yun Fat, Ringo Lam, Simon Yam) and articles (John Woo, *Moment Of Romance*, *Hard Boiled*). There are also 5 Special Editions and 2 video magazines with interviews and film clips. For more information contact Eastern Heroes, 96 Shaftesbury Avenue, London W1V 7DH. PD

The Essential Guide To Deadly China Dolls by Rick Baker & Toby Russell

Let's be plain about it - Femme Fatale movies are not subtle. Of the few that are available in the UK, the defining image is of actress Chingamy Yau, dressed only in leather hot pants and lipstick, tits oot, pump action shotgun in hand (fnaar, fnaar). The image, originally intended as publicity fodder for the film *Naked Killer*, has become ubiquitous when discussing Femme Fatale movies. Rick Baker and Toby Russell's tome on the subject *The Essential Guide To Deadly China Dolls* uses her on both the front and back covers, as well as at every possible opportunity in-between. Why not? The image is, after all, representative of the genre which only has two themes - sex and violence. Or, more properly, sexual violence.

Wong Jing, director of successes *City Hunter* and *God Of Gamblers*, turned his hand to Category III movies by producing *Naked Killer*. If this had been a tale about hitmen and their mixed-up emotions, it would have featured a lot of drinking, constant smoking, maybe a little saxophone playing, and extensive shootouts. As it is, it concerns hitwomen, and therefore centres more on fits of pique, lesbian bath scenes (always a favourite of Japanese anime) and assassins who insist on having sex with their prey before killing them. Funny how Chow Yun Fat never seemed moved to ask, "So, you want a quick shag before I blow your head off?"

The mainstream Hong Kong action movies, where women are the victims or subplots but almost never the subjects, focus on loyalty and on the bond that can join two sworn adversaries if both comply with their own ethical systems. They are about the nobility that can rise from the carnage of physical violence. They are, in other words, about heroes. They're also about finding neat ways of killing people.

Given the inherent sexism of most paternalistic cultures, it doesn't come as any great surprise to find that women, by and large, are not portrayed as heroes. If women resort to violence it is seen as a weakness. Consequently, with the recent proliferation of Cat III films in Hong Kong, women have been promoted to subject matter wholly and solely because this affords an opportunity to explore their lack of personal morality. A man with a machine gun is a hero who kills out of moral outrage or self-defence; a woman with an uzi is a whore who kills out of infantile jealousy and spite.

Sex and sexuality are subjects which almost never feature in mainstream (usually Cat II) action movies, yet they are usually the main concern of their Femme Fatale Cat III contemporaries. When the Hong Kong film industry was flush with money it produced glossy high-concept pieces like *Hard Boiled*. Now it is scratching round for pennies, it produces cheap and nasty movies with low concepts or no concepts. It is difficult to look for higher ideals in a film when the title character has stripped down to a basque and g-string to make a feminist statement by blowing her attacker's dick off.

When Russ Meyer or Pedro Almodovar wander into this territory they are there to massage the intellect as well as the libido - theirs are films you can study and explore and discuss, as well as jerk off to. Not so the Cat III films - they are designed to be used once then disposed of, slightly soiled. This is a shame because, particularly in the case of *Naked Killer* and *Deadly China Dolls*, the two primary releases in this sub-genre, the production values are high enough to stand these films against any of their male-orientated forebears. The problem lies in the simple-mindedness of the story and the unquestioning, indefensible exploitation of women.

It is unusual for a Cat III film to be released in the UK, and almost unheard of for one to hit the high streets uncut. *Naked Killer* achieved this rare feat, which may also partly explain why it is the flagship for these films. However, a more common fate befell the delightfully entitled *Escape From Brothel* which was cut to ribbons upon its release by Eastern Heroes. Howard Lake, in the aforementioned *Essential Guide* describes the original version as featuring "...privations inflicted upon its two female protagonists that were strong stuff by anyone's standards...sex scenes combined with moments of jaw-dropping unpleasantitude (sic), in which electrocution and a baseball bat figure heavily, further indicating a demand for pictures to provide more raw meat upon which audiences could chew." (pp 247-249)

This says two things to me: firstly, as with the death-throes of the English film industry in the late 60s and early 70s, pornography is the last ditch attempt to milk money from a market that no longer pays attention. Obviously, *The Confessions Of A Window Cleaner* hardly rates as hardcore, but is as close as legitimate film making is ever likely to get in the UK. So the upsurge of Cat III in Hong Kong is the proof, if the exodus of its directing and acting talent weren't proof enough, of the death of the indigenous Hong Kong film industry.

Secondly, and more troublingly, I am aware that by reporting on films like *Escape From Brothel* I will be contributing to a lascivious market for them. In common with the Italian exploitation movies of the 70s and 80s, which threw up such 'notable' names as Lucio Fulci and Dario Argento (who, to my continuing amazement, now seems to have achieved the status of artist in the eyes of some critics) as well as many names which have, thankfully, faded back into obscurity; the recent trend in cheap, exploitation movies being churned out under the Cat III banner is destined for cult status and black market collectibility.

Despite their flagrant and almost total lack of artistic merit, films like *Driller Killer* (1979, dir Abel Ferrara) and *Zombie Flesh-Eaters* (1979, dir Lucio Fulci) are still a fixation for a certain sector of (generally male and teenage) society. Owning the largest collection of banned videos becomes a badge of achievement, not because you like or even watch the films, but simply because you've successfully bucked the system by owning them. I do not think that it would do the serious appreciation of Hong Kong cinema, from the slapstick of Jackie Chan to the circumspection of Wong Kar-Wai, any good whatsoever to be tarred with the brush which will, invariably, be used in a futile attempt by the moral 'majority' to obliterate Cat III from Britain's top shelves. In no way do I support censorship, but I sometimes have to wonder if upholding the right-to-be-seen of a few cheap, tacky porno-schlock movies is worth the inevitable price in the knee-jerk banning of worthier, more substantial movies.

This isn't an issue which troubles the producers of *The Essential Guide To Deadly China Dolls*, however. The book sets out to be an exhaustive appreciation of all the cheesecake stars of all the Femme Fatale movies, and a list of the films they've made (although, I think including *Chungking Express* was a bit tenuous, guys!) As a source book, it succeeds admirably. At one point it lists the earnings of the top 20 actresses, which points out quite plainly that they may be exploited on screen, but they're getting very rich off it.

My problem with the book is in the leering, salacious language the 'lads' responsible have employed throughout. They certainly know their subject, and want us to know about it too, but the schoolboy humour that tinges practically every page only contributes to the indignity. At the end of his introduction, Jonathan Ross states that, one day, purchasers of this book will stop drooling over the hundreds and hundreds of pictures and actually start to read the text. That's if they haven't gone blind by then.

So we have a laddish 'appreciation' of female action movies which is depressingly predictable in its tone. Isn't it about time we read a piece stating the female perspective on these films and, for that matter, on the male-orientated action movies which preceded them? I think it is! Ladies, consider the gauntlet thrown. JA

Hong Kong Action Cinema by Bey Logan, 1995, Titan Books, £14.99

To those of us who are not au fait with Hong Kong's culture, history and language, its films form a near impenetrable maze of unpronounceable names and sequels of sequels of remakes. This book sets out to shed light on it all and, as far as I am concerned, it is already indispensable.

Logan begins with the roots of the industry, before dealing with the major players one-by-one: such as Bruce Lee, Jackie Chan and John Woo, but not at the expense of the less-well-known (and therefore, to some extent, more interesting) figures.

So, this profusely illustrated and clearly laid-out book was made just for you if you don't know your Ko Fei from your Lau Kar Fai, and are blinded by the plethora of wonderful titles they come up with (anyone for *Pantyhose Hero* or *Eight Diagram Pole Fighter* or my own personal favourite: the positively poetic *Snake In The Eagle's Shadow*?)

Logan maintains a light, chatty style throughout, resisting analysis in favour of raw data - after all, this is a history of the genre, not a critique. However, how one researches an industry which is based in many countries throughout the South China Seas, with companies coming-into and going-out-of business with gay abandon; while the films they make are re-dubbed, re-cut and re-titled with production-line regularity, is beyond me. It is a real testament to the author's love of and dedication to the genre that the picture he paints is so coherent.

If you love action movies, want to venture into Hong Kong territory, but don't know where to start ... start here. Logan knows his subject, and after reading his book, so will you! JA

Hong Kong Babylon by Fredric Dannen & Barry Long, 1997, Faber & Faber, £12.99

At once illuminating and frustrating, it is divided into 4 sections. The introduction gives a good overview of the modern Hong Kong film industry. The plethora of interviews are far too short to give anything more than a taste of the main players being discussed - they interview Tsui Hark for 5 hours yet only publish a couple of quotes! The alphabetical list of movie reviews is by far the best aspect, in that I found movies not listed elsewhere, but coverage is far from in-depth. The final part is a list of the favourite Hong Kong films of 12 film critics. Although this may seem like a good idea, in practice all we get is a long list of film titles with little in the way of helpful criticism. For such a thick book, and for all the talent involved, this is a surprisingly quick read with little depth. PD

Sex And Zen & A Bullet In The Head by Stefan Hammond & Mike Wilkins, 1997, Titan Books, £12.99

This book is a guide to over 200 modern Hong Kong movies, the good and the bad, including many examples of badly translated subtitles like "Take my advice or I'll spank you without pants...!" The reviews are more in-depth than seen elsewhere, and there is lots of trivia to keep one amused. For this reason it wins out over *Hong Kong Babylon*. However, it is not as suffused with background knowledge and the years of history that is apparent in Bey Logan's *Hong Kong Action Cinema*. Still, the sections on John Woo, Ringo Lam, Hong Kong Noir, Off The Wall and Unpolished Fists will keep young bloodshedders amused. PD

You Want To Watch More?

Okay, you've read the reviews of the Heroic Bloodshed films available on video and you are looking for more. What do you do? Well, you have two choices.: first, you can visit www.easternheroes.co.uk to buy Eastern Heroes, MIA and Made In Hong Kong videos; second, you can go out and buy a VCD (that's a Video-CD) player and buy Hong Kong VCDs direct from your local Chinatown (e.g. CD News in London - 0171 287 2880), or go on the internet (try the shop at www.coolala.com). In many cases, VCDs will be the only way you get to see Heroic Bloodshed films.

Here is a list of more Heroic Bloodshed titles for you to hunt down - many of them are only available in VCD. They will often have Chinglish subtitles. Also, these are English versions of their titles, so they may bear little or no relation to the original Chinese name.

Arrest The Restless (1992)
Asian Cops: High Voltage (1995)
A Better Tomorrow III (1989)
The Big Heat (1988)
Black Cat (1991)
Black Cat II (1992)
Burning Ambition (1989)
Casino Raiders (1989)
City War (1989)
Dangerous Encounter Of The First Kind (1980)
Deception (1989)
Department O (1994)
Dr Lamb (1992)

Eastern Condors (1986)
Easy Money (1987)
The Final Option (1994)
Final Victory (1987)
Full Trottle (1995)
Gangs (1987)
Gunmen (1988)
Gun-N-Rose (1992)
Hard To Kill (1992)
Hero Of Tomorrow (1988)
Hunting List (1994)
The Incorruptible (1993)
Killer's Romance (1989)
Legacy Of Rage (1986)

Long Arm Of The Law (1984)

Long Arm Of The Law II (1987)

Long Arm Of The Law III (1989)

Love Among The Triad (1993)

Love And The City (1994)

Love, Guns And Glass (1995)

Love Massacre (1981)

Loving You (1995)

My Heart Is That Eternal Rose (1989)

Naked Killer (1992)

Night Caller (1985)

On The Run (1987)

Organised Crime And Triad Bureau (1993)

Passion (1995)

Passion Unbounded (1995)

Peace Hotel (1995)

Police Confidential (1995)

Pom Pom And Hot Hot (1992)

Red Shield (1991)

Sexy And Dangerous (1996)

Soul (1986)

The Story Of Woo Viet (1981)

Taxi Hunter (1993)

Tiger Cage (1988)

To Be Number One (1991)

Treasure Hunt (1994)

What A Wonderful World (1995)

Internet Sites

There are many internet sites covering every aspect of Hong Kong cinema, and few of them specifically deal with Heroic Bloodshed. Here are a few places for you to look for more info. Virtually all of these sites link into 20 or more other sources, so make sure you have the permission of the phone bill payer before commencing your surf. Beware of alternative film titles and cast & crew names, also many sites can be in Chinese.

Hong Kong Movie Database - http://www.hkmdb.com/ - latest news/reviews, start here, it's great

Action Web - http://www.geocities.com/Hollywood/6648/index.html - the best John Woo/ Tsui Hark site I could find, and it has an enormous links page

Hardboiled - http://www.hardboiled.de/ - dedicated to John Woo

For A Few Bullets More - http://home2.swipnet.se/~w-20851/hemsida/ - John Woo site

Bullet In The Web - www.johnwoo.com - John Woo site

What Do We Have Here - http://www.xs4all.nl/~chinaman/ - great site all about Wong Kar-Wai, with news/links/interviews but doesn't seem to have been updated recently

Hong Kong Film Magazine - http://www.hkfilmmag.com/ - has Ringo Lam special issue

Hong Kong Film Critics - http://filmcritics.org.hk/ - HK critics give their views on the latest releases

Australian Heroic Cinema - http://www.heroic-cinema.com/ - catch up on down under

Hong Kong Cinema - http://egret0.stanford.edu/hk/

Hong Kong Movieworld - http://www.movieworld.com.hk/

Hong Kong Videos Links - http://mdstud.chalmers.se/hkmovie/

You can talk to other people interested in Asian cinema, at top newsgroup alt.asian-movies.

The Essential Library

If you've enjoyed this book why not try the following titles in the Pocket Essentials library?

The Slayer Files: Buffy the Vampire Slayer by Peter Mann - Complete episode guide and cast information on the hit TV series of the millennium featuring the most beautiful girl on the planet.

Woody Allen by Martin Fitzgerald – Follow his life from desperate comedian to tragic dramatist.

Jackie Chan by Michelle Le Blanc & Colin Odell (March 2000) – Every broken bone dissected, every stupendous stunt analysed, and every action movie reviewed.

The Brothers Coen by John Ashbrook & Ellen Cheshire – The curious charm of the modern Brothers Grimm, from *Blood Simple* to *The Big Lebowski*.

Film Noir by Paul Duncan (April 2000) – Films of trust and betrayal, from *Double Indemnity* to *Touch Of Evil*.

Heroic Bloodshed edited by Martin Fitzgerald (March 2000) – Hong Kong Action Cinema, where only the bullets are faster than the subtitles! Features interviews with John Woo and Wong Kar-Wai.

Alfred Hitchcock by Paul Duncan – He spent his life creating public unease with *Psycho*, *Vertigo*, *Rear Window* and 50 more films. Find out how Hitch did it.

Stanley Kubrick by Paul Duncan – *Eyes Wide Shut* was only the latest in a long line of controversial films by the director's director.

David Lynch by Michelle Le Blanc & Colin Odell – Close your minds to the surreal, violent world of *Twin Peaks* and *Wild At Heart*. Open your hearts to the beauty of *The Elephant Man* and *The Straight Story*.

Noir Fiction by Paul Duncan (April 2000) – On your travels down the dark highways of fiction you will meet James M Cain, Cornell Woolrich, Jim Thompson, David Goodis, Charles Willeford, James Ellroy, Derek Raymond and many troubled souls.

Orson Welles by Martin Fitzgerald – He made the best American film ever made, *Citizen Kane*, and then got better! Discover how.

Available at all good bookstores at £2.99 each, order online at **www.pocketessentials.com**, or send a cheque to:

Pocket Essentials (Dept HB), 18 Coleswood Rd, Harpenden, Herts, AL5 1EQ, UK

Please make cheques payable to 'Oldcastle Books.' Add 50p postage & packing for each book in the UK and £1 elsewhere.

US customers should contact Trafalgar Square Publishing on 802-457-1911 (Tel), 802-457-1913 (Fax), e-mail: tsquare@sover.net